Crossing Boundaries
The Deployment of Global IT Solutions

Rosann Webb Collins
University of South Florida

Laurie J. Kirsch
University of Pittsburgh

Practice-Driven Research in IT Management Series™
Madeline Weiss and Robert W. Zmud, Editors
www.pinnaflex.com/apc

Cover design: Kevin Cox, Custom Editorial Productions, Inc.
Production coordination: JaNoel Lowe, Custom Editorial Productions, Inc.

This book was set in Times Roman by Custom Editorial Productions, Inc., Cincinnati, Ohio. It was printed and bound by Malloy Lithographing, Inc., Ann Arbor, Michigan.

ISBN:1-893673-01-4

CONTENTS

List of Figures

List of Tables

CHAPTER 1

INTRODUCTION

More and more businesses are implementing global information technology (IT) solutions. These solutions are meant to support global business activities for companies whose processes, staffs, markets, and customers are increasingly worldwide in scope. For many businesses, the deployment of a global IT solution represents new territory, and they have little, if any, past experience to use as a template. Moreover, because the deployment of global IT solutions is relatively recent, there are few industrywide accepted practices or guidelines for individual businesses to draw on.

Exacerbating the lack of accepted practices or guidelines is the unique nature of global (versus domestic) IT solutions. Development and implementation processes for these global projects present many challenges. Some of these challenges are internal to the business. For example, the project team must not only understand the unique local needs of individual business units but also reconcile those with the overall global needs of the company itself. The project team might also be distributed around the globe, and coordinating their work activities can be a formidable task. Other challenges are external to the business. One such challenge is the lack of a robust IT infrastructure in some parts of the world. Another is the scarcity of local technical expertise to build and support a global IT solution. These challenges not only make it difficult to initially implement the solution but also impede the long-term viability of the solution.

Managing and overcoming these challenges can prove daunting. There are, however, some businesses that have experience with the deployment of global IT solutions. Some of these experiences have been successful, and some have not. By examining the approaches taken, we can identify and develop useful insights and guidelines for practice.

Overview of Research Project

In this book, we report on the experiences of several businesses and their efforts to deploy global IT solutions. In particular, we address two broad questions.

Question 1: What Are Global IT Solutions?
To answer this question, we investigated several specific issues:
- What makes an IT solution "global"?
- What is driving the deployment of the global IT solution?
- What outcomes are anticipated from deploying global IT solutions? How is success viewed and measured?
- What development and implementation approaches are used to deploy global IT solutions?

Question 2: What Are Successful Practices for Deploying Global IT Solutions?
Here, we examined the following topics:
- What processes and techniques are used to develop, implement, and maintain global IT solutions?
- How does the deployment process differ for global solutions?
- How are the activities of project team members and other stakeholders controlled and coordinated?
- How are changes across technologies, business processes, roles, and responsibilities managed?

Research Approach
We investigated these questions using a multiphased research design that included a literature search, telephone interviews, and in-depth case studies (see Chapter 2). From the literature review, we learned of some companies' experiences with deploying global IT solutions, as well as challenges they faced. Armed with this information, we developed some general insights into the nature of global IT solutions and difficulties with deploying them. To learn more, we conducted telephone interviews with senior management from eleven firms to explore specific deployment efforts. From these interviews we gained an understanding of the types of global solutions being deployed and of the broad set of issues associated with deploying global IT solutions. We then selected five companies to study in-depth. In this phase of the study, we focused on identifying specific challenges related to developing and implementing global IT solutions, as well as strategies and techniques for addressing these challenges.

Summary of Findings
In this section, we give an overview of our findings. We present our results in detail in Chapters 3–9.

Question 1: What Are Global IT Solutions?
Here we investigated four specific issues: What makes an IT solution global? What drives the deployment of global IT solutions? What outcomes are anticipated from deploying these solutions? What development and implementation approaches are used? The findings related to each issue are summarized here.

Issue A: What Makes an IT Solution Global? From our research, we derived the following definition. Global IT solutions are information technology–based systems that span geographic and other boundaries to support global business processes. They make take the form of
- Data, software, and/or hardware architectures,
- Single-function solutions with a global presence.
- Integrated solutions to support cross-functional and dispersed business processes.

Data, software, and hardware architectures represent one form of global IT solution. These solutions provide standardization across all units of a particular business. Such a solution may, for example, provide a standard way of viewing and accessing data companywide. This facilitates a company's efforts to manage a business process globally as it promotes a common understanding of data related to that business process. The initial goals behind the efforts of Air Products and Chemicals, Inc., to consolidate its U.S. and British data centers included cost savings and shared worldwide applications. Over time, however, the firm found that project ICON enabled global business processing by facilitating global communication, global engineering systems, and global access to data.[1]

A single-function solution with a global presence, the second form of global IT solution, is an IT application that supports a business process that spans geographic locations. Caterpillar, for example, is assembling a system that will monitor industrial equipment remotely and notify a local dealer when a part begins to show signs of wear or impending failure. The message to the dealer will include the machine's make and location, as well as sensor data, a diagnosis, and parts and tools needed to service the machine. The dealer can access a global system that links dealers, parts distribution warehouses, product factories (both Caterpillar's and its suppliers'), and large customers' inventory systems to determine the best location of the parts and times of delivery.[2] Northern Telecom Ltd. (Nortel) recently deployed a single functional global IT solution to support its human resources activities. The solution consists of a set of core global elements. Depending on a local business unit's needs, some subset of these elements is implemented, along with necessary local adaptations. While each unit decides what software to run, each is also responsible for ensuring that the data will flow smoothly into the corporate database.[3] In both examples, the solutions support one major global process: after-sales service for Caterpillar and human resources for Nortel.

The third form of global IT solution refers to those ***integrated IT applications that support cross-functional, dispersed business processes*** on a global scale. SAP, Peoplesoft, Baan, and Oracle provide these types of solutions. Bristol-Myers decided to implement SAP R/3 to link the software applications that support a variety of business processes, including accounting, inventory management, and manufacturing. Rather than having to manually integrate information about a single product (e.g., shampoo, cardboard) across disparate systems, Bristol-Meyers can now retrieve consolidated information from SAP R/3. The SAP global solution also lets Bristol-Meyers send its customers one invoice for all products; in the past, separate invoices were generated from the separate systems.[4]

Issue B: Drivers of Deployment. Global IT solutions are deployed for a number of reasons. In this research, we found five drivers. A primary driver for many firms is *cost reduction.* Another major driver is the *need for globally integrated information,* which allows data to be shared across business units and across geographies. For some firms, the driver to deploy a global IT solution is *customer expectations;* that is, customers demand a common "look and feel" or a single invoice or statement from the firm. The *recognition of common business processes or products* also drives the deployment of global IT solutions: Rather than supporting such processes or products with multiple IT solutions, one common solution can be built. Finally, *serendipity* plays a role in that some firms see the deployment of a global IT solution as a chance to address other existing IT–related problems.

Issue C: Deployment Outcomes and Success. Recognizing that "success" is multidimensional, firms that deploy global IT solutions hope to realize both tangible and intangible outcomes. These include meeting project schedule and budget criteria (tangible outcomes) and enabling the transformation to a global firm (intangible outcomes). While the intangible outcomes are difficult to precisely quantify and assess, they represent, for most firms, the more meaningful and desired set of outcomes.

Issue D: Development and Implementation Approaches. Firms that deploy global IT solutions must decide how the solution will be developed and implemented. Development choices range from purchasing packaged software to building in-house solutions. Some firms allow packaged software to be customized; others do not. In many instances, the solution is divided into "core" elements and "local" elements. Core elements are those modules of the solution that satisfy global firm needs and that are common to all locations. Local elements are those pieces that are adapted to local business unit needs.

Some firms rely heavily on external vendors for assistance with deploying global IT solutions, and others depend on in-house personnel.

The actual rollout or implementation of a global IT solution is complex because it typically requires changes to business processes as well as technology-based changes. Many firms establish implementation project teams that are distinct from the development project teams. These implementation teams may or may not include personnel from the local unit, but a successful rollout of a global IT solution requires the cooperation and commitment of users and managers from the local business unit.

Question 2: What Are Successful Practices for Deploying Global IT Solutions?
With this research question we focused on the processes of deployment, investigating how individuals can structure and manage efforts to deploy global IT solutions and the business changes that accompany those technology-based solutions. Our research findings suggest that to deploy global IT solutions, project team members and other project stakeholders have to cross four types of boundaries that exist within, between, and among companies: cultural, physical, structural, and technological.

Cultural boundaries are based on attitudinal and behavioral differences among groups of individuals. A group develops its own attitudes (e.g., toward authority) and norms for behaviors (e.g., how decisions are made) through common experience, education, and socialization. A culture may form in an office, a company, or a nation or on a continent.

Physical boundaries are based on real differences between business units: geographical location, time zone, language, currency, and legal and political environment.

Structural boundaries are based on differences among the function and level of business units within a company and among companies. Types of structural boundaries include those between centralized and decentralized units, between newly acquired business areas and the acquiring organization, and among different job categories.

Technological boundaries are based on differences in the hardware, software, data and network infrastructure; IS deployment methods and processes; and technological expertise available to a business unit. These boundaries emanate from the company and from the local environment.

Crossing each boundary represents a challenge to project stakeholders. Our study findings include a description of the deployment issues that stem from each of the four types of boundaries, as well as strategies and techniques for preventing or minimizing the problems these boundaries create. Challenges that arise from crossing the boundaries, and consequently the strategies and techniques for dealing with these issues, fall into four major themes: change management, control and coordination, knowledge management, and design choices.

Theme 1: Change Management. *Change management* refers to the process of implementing the myriad of changes accompanying the deployment of a global IT solution. Changes occur over time in businesses, teams, individuals, technology, and business processes. In the context of global IT solution deployment, the issues vary according to what is being changed (*focus* and *scope* of change), the *amount* of change, the *nature* of change (incremental or fundamental), and the *pace* of change.

Theme 2: Control and Coordination. Developing and implementing global IT solutions requires the coordinated effort of motivated individuals. Control mechanisms, such as compensation systems and challenging work assignments, are means of motivating individuals to achieve organizational objectives. Coordination mechanisms are ways to integrate various pieces of the solution and include steering committees and formal planning efforts. Because global IT solutions are often large, complex, and lengthy and because individuals are often located around the globe (sometimes in different organizations), control and coordination efforts require concerted thought and effort. Mechanisms that work for domestic IT projects may not be sufficient for global IT projects.

Theme 3: Knowledge Management. Knowledge in this context includes information and skills related to the deployment of global IT solutions that are stored in an individual's or an organization's knowledge base or in writing. Knowledge management includes the human resource issues of selection, training, and assignment and retention of knowledgeable and skilled individuals, documentation of knowledge, and the transfer of knowledge to individuals and the organization.

Theme 4: Design Choices. Deploying a global IT solution typically involves developing a complex solution with input from stakeholders in many regions of the organization and distributing a technology-based solution to different parts of the globe. It consequently requires IS and business managers and project teams to consider a range of technology options and to make tough choices about the development and installation of the solution. This scenario is often complicated by the fact that, for many firms, this is the first or a unique venture into global deployment; thus, there are few guidelines or templates available to aid the decision-making process.

How to Use This Book

Outline of Chapters

In Chapter 2, we describe the research design and methodology. In addition, we provide background information on the companies that participated in this research. In Chapter 3, we describe more fully the nature of global IT solutions, and we provide an overview of the challenges that businesses face as they deploy these solutions. We examine these challenges in depth in Chapters 4 through 7, where we discuss them in the context of crossing cultural, physical, structural, and technological boundaries. We organize these discussions around the four themes of change management, control and coordination, knowledge management, and design choices. In Chapter 8, we present a series of deployment timelines. These timelines identify the issues that can be addressed or monitored by CIOs and other senior managers during the project life cycle. In Chapter 9, we present a series of checklists. These contain specific action items for the project manager and team members to address during the project life cycle. We offer a few lessons learned and our concluding comments in Chapter 10.

Structure of the Book

Chapters 3 through 7 present full discussions of the nature of global IT solutions (Chapter 3) and the challenges that must be met to deploy those solutions (Chapters 4 through 7). The discussion in Chapter 3 is self-contained, in that the data supporting the text are presented in tables within the chapter. In Chapters 4 through 7, the issues raised in the deployment of global IT solutions are described in some detail. In addition, there are references to the case study data (in Appendix B) so that a reader can find additional information about how the issue was dealt with in a specific context.

In order to reduce the redundancy of information presented, Chapters 8 and 9 are not self-contained but reference other parts of the book for full treatment of issues listed. The Deployment Timelines in Chapter 8 present the deployment issues that should be addressed or monitored, arranged according to the stage in the project life cycle. While these prescriptions are discussed briefly, the reader is again given references to the case study data (in Appendix B) for additional information. The checklists in Chapter 9 are also arranged according to the stage in the project life cycle. Only the specific actionable items are listed, with references to Chapters 3 through 8 where the reader will find the details of activities and the rationale behind them.

The relationships among the parts of the book are depicted in Figure 1. The purpose of providing these linkages between sections is to allow the reader to easily find more detailed information, longer anecdotes about an issue, supporting evidence for the arguments made, and/or information from differing perspectives.

Figure 1. Organization of the Book

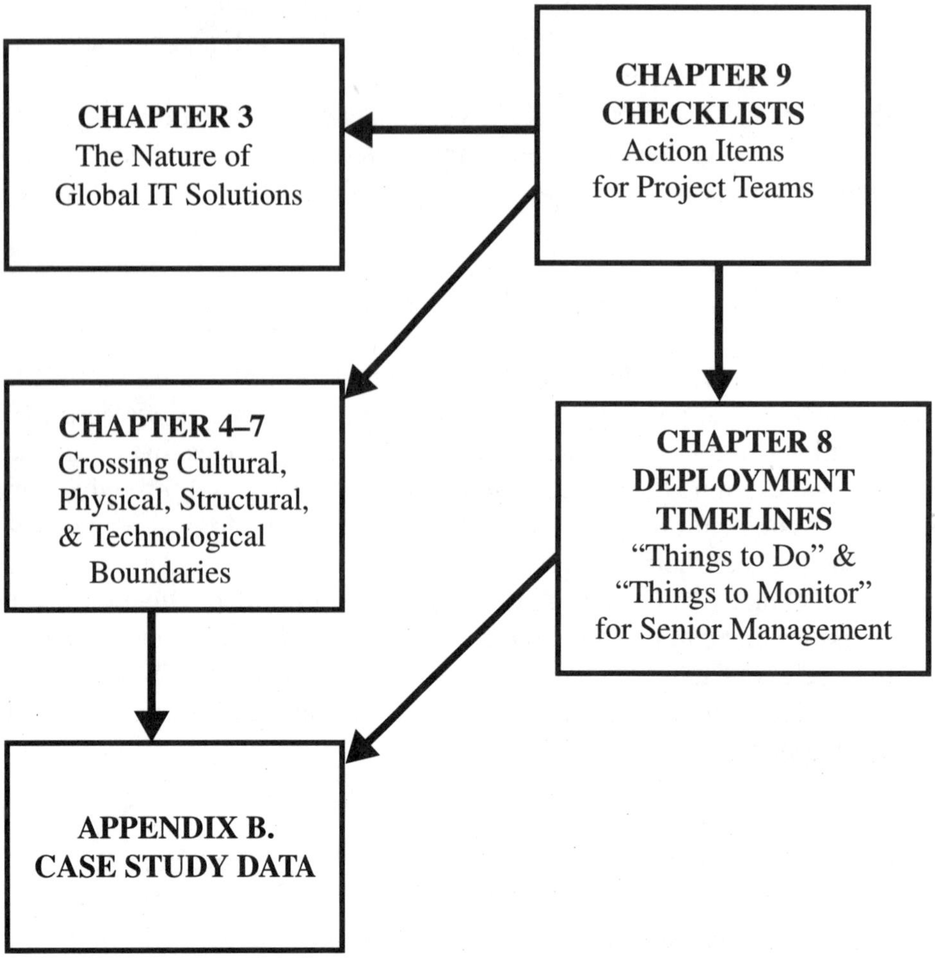

```
┌─────────────────────┐        ┌─────────────────────┐
│     CHAPTER 3       │◄───────│     CHAPTER 9       │
│    The Nature of    │        │    CHECKLISTS       │
│  Global IT Solutions│        │    Action Items     │
│                     │        │  for Project Teams  │
└─────────────────────┘        └─────────────────────┘
                          ╲              │
                           ╲             │
                            ▼            ▼
┌─────────────────────┐        ┌─────────────────────┐
│    CHAPTER 4–7      │        │     CHAPTER 8       │
│   Crossing Cultural,│        │    DEPLOYMENT       │
│ Physical, Structural,│       │     TIMELINES       │
│  & Technological    │        │   "Things to Do" &  │
│    Boundaries       │        │ "Things to Monitor" │
└─────────────────────┘        │ for Senior Management│
          │                    └─────────────────────┘
          │                      ╱
          ▼                     ╱
┌─────────────────────┐◄───────
│    APPENDIX B.      │
│  CASE STUDY DATA    │
└─────────────────────┘
```

Endnotes

[1]For more information, see the Harvard Business School cases written in 1992 and 1994 about Project ICON: Air Products and Chemicals, Inc.: Project ICON (A), (B), (C), and (D).

[2]More details about Caterpillar can be found in the 1996 *Harvard Business Review* article by Donald V. Fites.

[3]See the articles by Richard Butt (1995) and Samuel Greengard (1995) for more information about Nortel's global solution.

[4]For more information about Bristol-Myers, see the 1997 article in *Computerworld* by Randy Weston.

CHAPTER 2

RESEARCH DESIGN AND METHODOLOGY

To investigate the nature of global IT solutions and the way in which they are deployed, we conducted a field study between 1996 and 1998. The study was divided into three major phases: a literature review, a series of telephone interviews with senior management, and five in-depth case studies. The literature review and telephone interviews were intended to address the first broad research question: What are global IT solutions? The major focus of the case studies was the second research question: What are successful practices for deploying global IT solutions?

Phase 1: A Literature Review

We searched the academic and practitioner literature to find examples of global IT solutions. Our intent was to gain a better understanding of these solutions and to learn which companies had experience deploying these solutions. We were particularly interested in distinguishing between worldwide solutions (i.e., the same system is implemented in multiple locations) and global solution (i.e., a solution intended to support a distributed, global business process). We found a number of examples of global IT solutions in the literature.[1] However, few of these stories had much detail or richness, so they were not able to shed much light on our research questions. We therefore moved on to the next phase of our research.

Phase 2: Telephone Interviews

We supplemented our reading of the literature with a set of telephone interviews. To gain an overall understanding of the nature of global IT solutions, we focused on the following areas of interest:

- Types of global IT solutions deployed: What makes an IT solution "global"?
- Motivations for deployment: What are the drivers for deploying global IT solutions?
- Outcomes of deployment: What is the set of realized and anticipated outcomes from deploying global IT solutions? How is success viewed and measured?
- Approaches to deployment: What development and implementation choices are feasible and effective?

Our intent was to get a broad perspective on these issues by gathering information from a variety of firms from a diverse set of industries. We therefore decided to conduct telephone interviews of IS and business managers of firms that had recently completed deploying a global IT solution or who were currently deploying such a solution.

To meet the goals of this phase of the research, we contacted approximately thirty companies by letter, soliciting their participation. Eleven companies that had recently deployed global IT solutions or were currently embarking on them agreed to participate. We conducted fifteen telephone interviews, each lasting between 30 and 60 minutes, with managers from these companies. The interviews were structured and focused on the four issues articulated earlier. The interview protocol can be found in Appendix A.

A breakdown of the number of interviews conducted, according to organizational title, is shown in Table 1.

Table 1. Telephone Interviews Conducted, by Title

TITLE	NUMBER OF INTERVIEWS CONDUCTED
CIO / VP / Senior VP	7
IS Manager / Director	6
Functional Area Manager / Director	2
TOTAL:	15

The firms represent several industries, as depicted in Table 2.

Table 2. Telephone Interviews Conducted, by Industry

INDUSTRY	NUMBER OF FIRMS
Banking	1
Chemicals	2
Computer & DP Services	1
Food Processing	1
Health Care	2
Manufacturing & Processing	3
Transportation	1
TOTAL:	11

In terms of 1996 revenues, firm size ranged from about $2 billion to $25 billion. Total number of employees (worldwide) varied between approximately 13,500 and 145,000.

Phase 3: In-Depth Case Studies

The intent of the third phase of this research was to delve into issues of deployment more deeply. While the goal of the previous phases was broad coverage, focusing on the nature of global IT solutions, the goal of the third phase was in-depth investigation, with a lens on understanding the deployment process. Four research questions motivated the second phase of the research:

- What approaches are used to develop, implement, and maintain global IT solutions?
- How does the deployment process differ for global solutions?
- How are the activities of project team members and other stakeholders controlled and coordinated?
- How are changes across technologies, business processes, roles, and responsibilities managed?

Case Descriptions

To investigate these questions, we conducted five case studies of global IT projects at five different companies. The projects and companies are briefly described here.

Case 1: Shipments. The Shipments project is under development at a multibillion-dollar firm in the shipping and logistics industry. The company, with worldwide headquarters in the United States, employs over 100,000 individuals. The purpose of the Shipments projects is to facilitate import and export processing of global shipments. This global IT solution is a custom-developed application that is enterprisewide in scope; it affects nearly every business unit. The primary business driver for the Shipments project is reducing the costs of import and export shipping. Not only is the firm interested in lowering business costs, but also it is striving to lower the costs of deploying IT solutions. This effort has impacted the design choices made for the Shipments project. The final deliverable will consist of a set of "core" global components that individual business units can "take off the shelf," integrate with existing local applications, make needed adaptations, and implement the resulting solution locally.

The development of Shipments is being done in pieces: the entire project was divided into eleven increments, each with its own schedule, budget, and set of project teams. There are multiple project teams associated with Shipments. In particular, there are a core global team and a technical and business team for each increment. The core global team includes a user liaison whose responsibility is to facilitate communication between the core team and the users in Europe, who will implement the first version of the firm increment.

Case 2: Production. The Production solution is in operation at a company that is a leader in health care supply distribution, manufacturing, and management services. This multibillion-dollar company, headquartered in the United States, has over 20,000 employees worldwide. The Production project centered on the installation of the integrated packaged software called *PRMS*. *PRMS* was implemented in multiple divisions; it supports, among other functions, accounts payable, general ledger, shop floor control, purchasing, and materials management. Primary business drivers for the Production project were cost reduction and improved data quality and flow.

PRMS was deployed in stages by business area. A separate project team was assembled to handle each deployment. The teams were cross-functional and cross-divisional, generally consisting of both systems and business personnel.

Case 3: Enterprise. The Enterprise project involves the implementation of all functions of SAP R/3 in all locations of a multibillion-dollar chemical company. The company is headquartered in the United States, and employs over 8,000 people worldwide. Recently, the firm has faced a significant financial crisis, which has fueled the urgency of the Enterprise project because significant financial gains are expected when the SAP R/3 implementation and accompanying reengineering efforts are completed. Key business drivers for this project include cost avoidance and reduction, as well as the move away from functionally oriented management and to global supply chain management.

There are multiple teams involved in the Enterprise project. A core global team, including both IS and business people, defines the global flows, develops functionality, and assists with local implementations. The local area teams are primarily responsible for their local adaptations and installations. Besides these project teams, there is a separate IT group that is responsible for the hardware infrastructure, data loading, and technical support.

Case 4: Metrics. The Metrics global IT solution is an infrastructure solution; it is the implementation of a data warehouse for one division within the company. A multibillion-dollar technology firm, the company employs more than 114,000 people worldwide. The primary purpose of the Metrics data warehouse is to provide operational and tactical repair delivery statistics on a specific range of technology products. In addition, the project was designed to demonstrate the efficacy of a new organizational unit that acted as a liaison between the IT unit and the business users.

Though the data warehouse was designed for one division, this division is global in scope, and therefore the Metrics solution impacts individuals around the globe. The core project team consists of people located around the world with development subteams in the United States and in the United Kingdom. Besides this team, there are local implementation teams and a team that is responsible for using the data warehouse to answer specific requests.

Case 5: Credit. The Credit system was developed by a large financial institution with headquarters in the United States and over 70,000 employees worldwide. Credit is intended to support a global letters-of-credit business process with activities and tasks spread around the world. This contrasts with the traditional view of letter-of-credit processing as a regional or local function. Interestingly, this project was initially viewed as a technology problem and solution, that is, as a problem of multiple systems written for multiple hardware platforms. It wasn't until the project was well under way that it was recognized as a way to reengineer the letters-of-credit processing and create a global business process.

The company explored the possibility of implementing packaged software, but it was unable to find a suitable solution. Instead, it decided to build a customized system using client/server technology. A core team was established at the U.S. headquarters. Implementation teams are assembled for each installation, these teams include people from the core team as well as local players. In addition, because responsibility for the global Credits project was originally located in Asia, a group of developers in Asia is responsible for local adaptations and implementations in Asia.

More detailed descriptions of each of the projects can be found in Appendix B. We selected these five companies for study because they have a record of successfully deploying IT solutions. In addition, we wanted variation in terms of the scope of the solution (from targeted to enterprisewide change efforts), the status of the solution (ongoing versus implemented), and type of solution (custom developed, package implementation, or infrastructure enhancement). As summarized in Table 3, the projects varied across these dimensions.

Table 3. Case Study Project Descriptions

PROJECT	SCOPE	STATUS	TYPE
Shipments	Enterprisewide	Ongoing	Custom developed
Production	Targeted (multiple divisions)	Implemented	Package
Enterprise	Enterprisewide	Pilots implemented; ongoing	Package
Metrics	Targeted (one division)	Early version implemented; ongoing	Infrastructure
Credit	Targeted (one business unit)	Majority of sites implemented; ongoing	Custom developed

Data Collection
The majority of the data were collected via interviews of IS and business unit managers as well as project team members and leaders. The interviews were semistructured and designed to address the research questions noted previously. The interview protocols are shown in Appendix A.

Most interviews were conducted on-site, either face to face (thirty-five interviews) or via teleconferencing (two interviews). A few additional interviews were conducted over the phone. Table 4 presents a breakdown of the number of interviews conducted for each case study, by organizational positions of the participants.

Table 4. Case Study Interviews

POSITION	SHIPMENTS	PRODUCTION	ENTERPRISE	METRICS	CREDIT
IS managers	2[a]		1	2	1
Business managers			2	1	
Project manager	1[b]	1[c]	1[c]		1
User liaison	1			1	
Team members	2	1	8	3	2
Support persons	2		2		1
End-users		1[d]		1	
TOTAL	8	3	14	8	5

[a]Two follow-up interviews were conducted (3 and 6 months after the original data were collected) with the manager of the technical staff to get updates on the project status.

[b]The project manager in this case is the business sponsor of the project. He is a part of the formal user liaison organization, and his background is in the business (as opposed to IT).

[c]The project managers in these cases come from the business (versus the IT) side of the organization.

[d]This interview was conducted on the phone.

Endnote
[1]Some of the examples we found are described in King (1996), Fryer (1996), Konsynski and Karimi (1993), Appleby (1992), Ives and Jarvenpaa (1994), Pitkanen (1990), Clemens, Row, and Miller (1992), and Sturken (1992).

CHAPTER 3

GLOBAL IT SOLUTIONS

The first general research question we considered was this: What are global IT solutions? We were particularly interested in four aspects of this question:

- What makes an IT solution "global"?
- What is driving the deployment of the global IT solution?
- What outcomes are anticipated? How is success viewed and measured?
- What development approaches are used to build and implement global IT solutions?

What Makes an IT Solution Global?

Global IT solutions are applications that support global business processes. They differ from other information technology–based systems in that the business processes they support or facilitate are distributed globally. Global IT solutions enable the operations of global firms, which are different from multinational companies. A multinational company is based in one host company with at least one foreign affiliate or production facility while global firms compete on a worldwide basis with production and/or service delivery processes that span multiple countries.

Global IT solutions span geographic and other boundaries to support these global business processes. We found that they take one of three forms:

- Data, software, and/or hardware architectures.
- Single-function solutions with a global presence.
- Integrated solutions to support cross-functional dispersed business processes.

Architectural solutions include infrastructure choices for software, hardware, and data. Installing a standard desktop configuration for every person in the firm is one example of an architectural solution. This form of global IT solution not only provides a standard means for utilizing information technology but also lays the foundation for the development of specific global applications. For example, one company (Firm 6, described in Tables 5, 6, 7, and 9 in this chapter) deployed 30,000 workstations with a standard configuration and applications, along with centralized IS functions and data centers, in order to provide a common platform for global databases and applications. In addition, Firm 6 realized considerable cost savings from volume purchasing and less complex support.

A single-function global IT solution allows a business process to be distributed globally. For example, a manufacturing solution might enable a firm to shift the production of a widget from a factory in Brazil to a factory in Taiwan based on existing capacity and resources. Sometimes the inherent nature of the business process is global, for example, global shipping. MSAS Cargo International developed its own logistics management information system to manage customers' airfreight.[1] This system helps efficiently manage shipments in accordance with a profile unique to each of MSAS's 25,000 customers. In addition, the system provides extensive feedback to customers on logistics performance and value-added services such as insurance, shipment packing and consolidation, customs work, and currency management. Another example is a bank (Firm 3, described in Tables 5, 6, 7, and 9 in this chapter) that made a decision to present a single "look and feel" to the customer worldwide. This decision was enabled by a custom-developed global IT solution.

Enterprisewide solutions expand the concept of single-function solutions by providing integrated support for several business processes, any or all of which might be distributed globally. Enterprise resource planning (ERP) packages such as SAP R/3 and Baan are examples of enterprisewide global IT solutions. Linking a wide range of business processes (e.g., ordering, manufacturing, purchasing, planning, accounting, and human resources), these solutions provide seamless integration of data across the firm. A real advantage to adopting ERPs is that these packages usually assume global operations and therefore have built-in functionality to handle multiple languages and currencies, as well as country-specific rules. For example, the human resources component of SAP R/3 supports extensive and varied benefits processing, which are needed for companies whose operations span many countries. In some situations, a firm may believe it does not have the internal resources and skills necessary to develop such a high functionality global solution (e.g., Firm 2, described in Tables 5, 6, 7, and 9 in this chapter). ERPs can also provide a mechanism for unifying recently merged or acquired business units. In the case of one manufacturing company (Firm 1, described in Tables 5, 6, 7, and 9 in this chapter), which was formed by the merger of two companies, the adoption of an enterprisewide integrated package became a way to combine business processes, rules, and procedures to complete the merger as well as to support continued global expansion of operations.

Table 5 presents additional examples of these three types of global IT solutions. For each of the eleven firms participating in the second phase of the research, the table descriptions detail the global IT solution and categorize the solution into one of the three forms: an architectural solution, a single-function solution, or an enterprisewide solution.

Table 5. Descriptions of Global IT Solutions

FIRM	SOLUTION	BACKGROUND & DESCRIPTIONS OF SOLUTIONS
1	Enterprisewide	Many current IT applications, which tend to be localized and site specific, span different business activities. These systems are no longer considered viable in a global economy. Firm 1, therefore, decided to deploy an enterprisewide integrated package to implement common solutions across geographies. This package is the firm's first deployment of a global IT solution.
2	Enterprisewide	Traditionally, applications in this firm have been built for each functional area or country or business unit. The result is that the same business process has been automated in various ways; thus it is now difficult to get globally integrated information about products, customers, suppliers, etc. To address this need for integrated information, Firm 2 has decided to implement SAP R/3 worldwide. The choice of SAP R/3 was made after determining that other packages on the market could not meet the functionality requirements and that the firm did not have the internal resources and skills necessary to develop the solution internally.

3	Single function	Having recently merged with another company, Firm 3 is still trying to merge and consolidate business processes and technologies. This turmoil affects IT functions as people and technologies are constantly on the move. The IT solution studied enables global letter-of-credit processing and replaces existing applications. While the project was ongoing, the project team recognized the need for business process reengineering; by redesigning the business process, the team was able to make the process more efficient and effective. The reengineering effort was thus driven by the project team.
4	Enterprisewide	Firm 4 adopted and adapted JD Edwards' integrated package with AS/400 systems.
5	All forms	One part of Firm 5's business is to develop and operate custom global IT solutions for its customers. No specific system was discussed in the interviews, but the interviewees discussed several solutions.
6	Architecture	This global IT solution involved the deployment of hardware, software, and support infrastructure. Firm 6 standardized workstation hardware and software around the globe, including a standard desktop and laptop, standard electronic mail and personal productivity software, and global customer service help desk. Roughly 30,000 workstations were deployed over the course of this project.
7	Enterprisewide	Firm 7 has typically developed applications in-house rather than purchase packages. As the firm grew internationally, the corporate IT unit responded to specific local needs with separate systems. Consequently, Firm 7 had developed similar applications for multiple locations. This global IT solution represents an effort to develop one common system that can be customized for different locations. The solution is intended to support import and export processing on a global basis.
8	Architecture	About three years ago, Firm 8 began to transform itself into a global organization. An IT infrastructure (i.e., computing and telecommunications capabilities) was put in place to support that transformation.
9	Architecture	Firm 9 is very decentralized, with affiliates throughout the world. Three technologies are coordinated on a global basis: voice network, data network, and data center. Firm 9 has standardized several technologies, including office automation, electronic mail, and data communication.
10	Enterprisewide	This firm is divided into four major business units, each of which has its own IT unit. At a corporate level, Firm 10 identifies business processes that are fairly standard and corresponding IT applications that are therefore "potentially sharable." A concerted effort is made to standardize these applications. One such application is Oracle Financials. The use of this package is not mandated to the business units, but "sold" to them on the basis of the package's advantages.
11	Enterprisewide	Firm 11 has grown by mergers and acquisitions, and has therefore acquired a myriad of business processes and systems, many of which are interrelated and quite complex. One such process and one system are logistics and related business processing. To deploy the logistics global IT solution, Firm 11 could either automate the complexity of the business process or streamline the company, changing the way the business process was conducted. The firm decided that it was not possible to automate the complexity but instead chose to simplify and streamline the logistics, sales, and manufacturing business processes.

What Drives the Deployment of Global IT Solutions?

A variety of environmental conditions motivates the deployment of global IT solutions. These have to do with the desire for improved internal efficiencies, the need to support increasing globalization, and the ability to meet customer expectations. In Table 6, we describe the motivation for the global IT solutions we studied.

Table 6. Motivating the Deployment of Global IT Solutions

FIRM	SOLUTION	MOTIVATION FOR GLOBAL IT SOLUTION
1	Enterprisewide	There are three motivations: (a) customers, who are global in scope, expect global IT solutions but not multiple order-entry interfaces, invoices, etc.; (b) a global firm needs globally integrated information; and (c) the year 2000 problem has to be addressed.
2	Enterprisewide	The primary driver is the need for global and integrated information to support a change from a functionally oriented to a process-oriented firm.
3	Single function	Two goals motivated this project: (a) to replace old technology, especially in Asia and Europe and (b) to reengineer the letter-of-credit business process. With respect to the second point, Firm 3 implemented a global, process- (versus functionally) oriented business strategy and so wanted all customers, no matter where they are located, to interface with the firm in the same manner.
4	Enterprisewide	The JD Edwards integrated package was deployed for several reasons. This software-hardware combination was already in place in many business units. In addition, the package could handle the volume, and the technology was considered fairly simple and low risk. This made the solution lower cost and meant that fewer people had to be convinced to conform.
5	All forms	Solutions are custom developed for external customers; the motivation therefore depends on the customer. No particular solution but a range of solutions was discussed in the interviews.
6	Architecture	Firm 6 is a global company with highly integrated businesses and processes (e.g., a plant manufactures products for multiple businesses). There is a need for global databases and integrated information to run the businesses globally. Beyond that, Firm 6 has two types of products, which affect IT–related decisions. Some products are commodities, and thus the overwhelming motivation for deploying IT is cost control. For specialty products, the motivation is market driven (e.g., meeting customer expectations).
7	Enterprisewide	The primary driver for this solution is cost reduction. Firm 7 wants to reduce the costs of processing shipments. Achieving this goal means that the shipment process will be reengineered as the global IT solution is built. This firm also wants to reduce the cost of deploying IT solutions. As a result, the project team has defined a new method for deploying global IT solutions, and the team is defining and documenting relevant processes and techniques of deployment.
8	Architecture	As Firm 8 changed from a "firm with an international presence" to a global organization, a need for integrated information was recognized in order to run the business globally. Deploying global IT solutions facilitates Firm 8's ability to leverage manufacturing, brand names, and support functions.
9	Architecture	The business strategy at Firm 9 is to allow affiliates to cater to local consumer tastes. There are, therefore, few centralized functions or services. However, voice, data, and data center capabilities were centralized to contain costs, to enable growth, and to leverage the corporate buying power of the firm. This approach provides employees with access to computing everywhere.

10	Enterprisewide	The motivators for implementing Oracle Financials include more effective and flexible operations at the corporate level, cost reduction, and integrated information.
11	Enterprisewide	Because the growth of Firm 11 has come from mergers and acquisitions, there is a need to merge, consolidate, and streamline business processes and technologies. The motivation for this global IT solution was to facilitate changes and simplifications to a complex business process.

Across the participating firms, there are five forces driving the deployment of global IT solutions: need for integrated information, cost reduction, meeting customer expectations, common business processes or products, and serendipity. Most firms express several motivations, although many are able to articulate a primary driver. Each driver or force is shown in Figure 1 and elaborated here.

Figure 2. Forces Driving the Deployment of Global IT Solutions

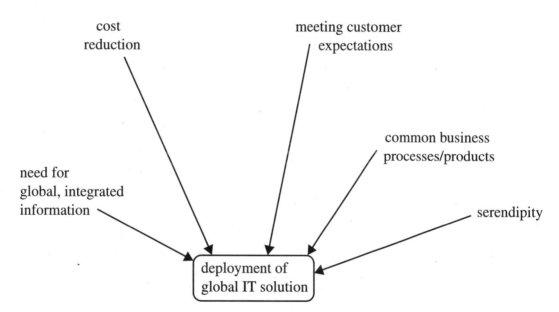

Several firms remarked that the primary motivation for the deployment of global IT solutions is the need for integrated information across geographies and across functional areas. These firms require the ability to manage products, suppliers, employees, and customers on a global basis. For many of these firms, existing applications had been built for a particular functional area, business unit, or geography; the amount of time and effort required to integrate data from these various applications is no longer acceptable. The need for global and integrated data drove the deployment of global infrastructure, enterprisewide integrated packages, and custom-developed applications.

For many firms, the primary driver for the deployment of global IT solutions is the need to reduce costs. This driver pertained mostly to infrastructure solutions. These firms typically see an opportunity to standardize on a set of hardware and software platforms, leveraging their buying relationships with vendors, and consequently driving down the costs of technology infrastructure. Interestingly, several firms remarked that it is possible to "recentralize" infrastructure because employees now recognize the difficulties inherent in communicating with others and sharing information when each firm unit utilizes different electronic mail systems, telecommunications networks, and other infrastructure technologies.

The need to meet customer expectations also drove the deployment of a particular global IT solution (though not an infrastructure solution). This need was manifested in one of two ways: (1) the desire to present external customers with the "same look and feel" no matter where in the world they interacted with the firm or (2) the desire to present industrial suppliers or customers with a common access to the firm. This latter factor is especially important when the supplier or customer is also a global firm.

Some firms found that common business processes or products were supported by different technology solutions. This situation had evolved over the years for one of two primary reasons. Some companies had traditionally built technological solutions for a particular location or functional area, responding to the needs of any one particular user group but not looking across areas to see where commonalities might exist. Other companies, which had experienced significant growth through mergers and acquisitions, inherited a plethora of IT solutions to address similar business processes or products. For these firms, therefore, a major driver for deploying global IT solutions was the desire to support common business processes or products with a single common system.

Finally, there were instances in which firms viewed the deployment of global IT projects as a serendipitous opportunity (from the standpoint of CIOs) to solve other IT problems. For example, a firm might see this deployment as a chance to build new systems that are free of the year 2000 problem rather than rewrite existing problematic systems.

What Outcomes Are Realized and Anticipated?

The drivers for deployment just discussed impact the type of outcomes anticipated by firms as they deploy global IT solutions. At the time of our research, some of the global IT solutions had been implemented and therefore outcomes were known. Other solutions were ongoing, however, so those outcomes are anticipated. In Table 7, we describe the anticipated and realized outcomes associated with the individual global IT solutions.

Table 7. Realized and Anticipated Outcomes of Deploying Global IT Solutions

FIRM	SOLUTION	ANTICIPATED & REALIZED OUTCOMES
1	Enterprisewide	At Firm 1, there is unanimous support among top management for the deployment of this global IT solution. Because top management feels this project is essential, there has been no hard cost justification for the project. There are, however, anticipated cost avoidance benefits: for example, problems in some existing systems do not have to be fixed because these systems will be replaced with the global IT solution. Perhaps the greatest anticipated outcome of this project, though, will be Firm 1's ability to present customers (especially global customers) with a common access to Firm 1.
2	Enterprisewide	The businesses want integrated data flows, and Firm 2 anticipates that this outcome will be achieved with the implementation of SAP R/3. Firm 2 also anticipates that individuals' ways of working will be changed as the orientation moves from local business functions to global business processes.

3	Single function	Realized outcomes include delivered functionality, significant use, demand for the new system, and elimination of the old system. There are some less-than-positive outcomes as well, including some less elegant aspects of the system and many difficulties arising from the use of leading-edge technology. Anticipated positive outcomes include the ability to install the solution in more geographies and to deliver it to additional users.
4	Enterprisewide	Firm 4 always views within-budget delivery of systems as a main criterion for success, and this project is on target to meet that goal. For this solution, expectations are high for full functionality and a nondisruptive implementation, because it is viewed as a low technology risk project.
5	All forms	Because Firm 5 develops global solutions for external clients, anticipated and realized outcomes differ.
6	Architecture	Firm 6 found it was able to leverage its size when purchasing hardware and software; it thus saved significantly more money than anticipated with the deployment of this global IT solution. This firm has been able to cost justify this infrastructure project because it keeps historical data related to the firm's unit set of costs. This particular project generated a high return in terms of costs. Other realized outcomes include facilitating global management by giving users the ability to plug in a laptop easily anywhere in the world. In addition, Firm 6 administered customer satisfaction surveys three weeks after the users received the workstations. It found that, overall, 88% of its users are satisfied or very satisfied, and only 12% are neutral or dissatisfied. Firm 6 has encountered little resistance to the project, which the interviewee believes is due, at least in part, to individuals' frustrations when trying to share and integrate data and to the project team's and top management's extensive and open communication about this infrastructure project. While Firm 6 was able to articulate some of the outcomes resulting from this project, the interviewee also commented that it is difficult to know the impact on users' work processes.
7	Enterprisewide	Firm 7 has articulated numerous success criteria. Some are related to the project itself—for example, more efficient processing. Others are related to the deployment process and include the extent to which the development process is repeatable.
8	Architecture	The deployment of this global IT solution enables communication and computing on a worldwide basis.
9	Architecture	Anticipated outcomes of the centralization effort were to reduce costs, to improve access to computing technologies, and to leverage the buying power of Firm 9.
10	Enterprisewide	Anticipated outcomes include more effective operations; integrated data, ability to more easily transfer employees, and cost savings. Another outcome is that the locations of some accounting jobs are changing from many sites to a few centralized locations. Unanticipated outcomes include the difficulties of working with leading-edge and untested technologies. Positive outcomes realized are successfully implementing Phase I within revised budget and schedule and the successful accommodation of major scope changes to the project.
11	Enterprisewide	Anticipated outcomes include streamlining complex business processes, the elimination of some jobs, and the need for new job skills. With the deployment of this global IT solution, Firm 11 also sees the need to change the way business is done.

The success of a global IT solution can be viewed in various perspectives. We found that firms thought about *product* success—that is, the extent to which the global solution met the specific needs and goals of the firms—as well as *process* success—the extent to which the deployment process met particular success criteria such as budget and schedule objectives. We summarize the various measures of success in Table 8.

Table 8. Measures of Success for Global IT Solutions

MEASURES OF SUCCESS	
Tangible	**Intangible**
Meeting project budget	Customer satisfaction
On-schedule delivery	Enabling transformation to global company
Functionality	Technical elegance
Reduction of infrastructure costs	Ability to add functionality
(unable to measure changes in work processes)	Ability to transport solution to other geographies
(unable to cost justify integrated package)	Meeting management expectations
	Meeting customer expectations

Many firms discussed the issue of "success" in both tangible and intangible terms. The tangible measures tend to reflect fairly traditional measures: on-time delivery, costs within budget, and delivered functionality. In addition, some of the firms deploying global infrastructure measured success in terms of lowered infrastructure costs. The tangible measures shown in parentheses indicate success measures that respondents said they were unable to measure, though they would have liked to.

The intangible measures are generally more difficult to quantify and thus more difficult to assess. The firms in this study generally described three types of intangible measures of success: those relating to top management perceptions of the global IT solution (e.g., whether the solution enables the transformation to a global company), those assessing internal and external customer reactions (e.g., customer satisfaction; meeting customer expectations), and those indicating the long-term viability of the technical solution (e.g., ability to add functionality in the future; ability to transport the solution to other geographies).

When discussing success, many of these firms recognized that success has multiple dimensions. No firm labeled a project as an "outright failure," though some of the projects were characterized as "less successful" (e.g., projects that were over budget, late, or that failed to produce an elegant technical solution). Some of these problems are direct results of the nature of deploying global IT solutions. For example, the time to negotiate with local IT and business units within the company can represent a considerable source of delay. Also, while technical problems with poor infrastructure might be anticipated, other problems with local regulation and cultural differences are likely to lead to unanticipated additional costs. Some problems are not unique to global IT solutions. For example, MSAS Cargo project described earlier experienced significant scope creep during development, and within five years costs ballooned from 9 million pounds to 21.

What Is the Development Approach?

Firms can develop and implement global IT solutions using a variety of approaches, techniques, and strategies. We found that some firms choose packaged software while others build the solution in-house. Firms differ with respect to how customized a solution can be for various business units. Implementation strategies and project team structures also varied. For implementation, identifying the person responsible for the implementation, the alignment of business and technological change, and the location of initial solution deployment were often three key decisions that were made. Project team structures were typically complex, reflecting the need for centralized effort to create a common global solution, while understanding and accommodating local needs. Teams included members from both IT and business units and from various geographical areas. In some cases, multiple teams were formed for specific aspects of deployment: a centralized team might create the core solution while regional teams might be responsible for local adaptation and/or implementation. The global nature of the solution in some cases exacerbated typical project team issues, such as difficulty in finding and retaining qualified personnel in all geographical areas, the additional costs to the firm and individuals from travel and co-location, and additional communication difficulties from language and cultural differences.

In Table 9, we summarize the development choices made by the eleven firms participating in the telephone interviews. In addition, deployment strategies and techniques are discussed in detail in Section III of each case study in Appendix B. The nature and success of these varied strategies and techniques are detailed in Chapters 4–7, where they are presented in the context of the specific global boundaries being crossed.

Table 9. Development Choices for Deploying Global IT Solutions

Firm	Solution	DEPLOYMENT CHOICES		
		Development	Implementation	Project Team Structure
1	Enterprisewide	Package installation	Rollout by region, with first implementation in two regions (Canada and Europe) simultaneously	• Core team of six people from HQ • Local teams for implementation • Global manager
2	Enterprisewide	SAP R/3 installation	Separate implementations in Europe and the United States; use of multiple pilot sites	• Global steering committee • Regional councils • Business unit teams • Reengineering process teams • Matrix structure between business units and reengineering teams
3	Single function	In-house, custom-developed application; client/server technology	Rollout began with 5 locations in Asia, followed by Europe, and then North America	• Asian project team supplemented with consultants began effort • Development effort shifted back to U.S. headquarters • Global committee and three-person team representing the United States, Europe, and Asia responsible for functional requirements • Steering committee
4	Enterprisewide	?	The package and platform were selected because they were already common in the organization, so new adaptation began in those sites	• Standing steering committee (all CIO's direct and dotted-line reports) • Purchased standard package adapted by global team (IS + local business unit users)

5	All forms	?	?	• Always use local team for development and on-going support • In some countries government regulation forces use of separate company as provider
6	Architecture	Standard desktop and laptop hardware (four IBM–compatible machines) and Microsoft software	Rollout began with an integrated product test with 120 users. Within 9 months it was 80% complete, with 23,000 PCs installed around the globe. Then a more gradual rollout of remaining 7000 was undertaken for rest of company	• Overall project manager • 21 direct reports with separate responsibilities • IS professionals + full-time person from Public Affairs + four or five full-time functional area users • 60% of staff located in U.S. global HQ; remainder from around globe
7	Enterprisewide	Custom-developed application with "core" elements and "local" elements	First rollout will be in United Kingdom, the sponsor for the project; other rollouts not yet decided upon Core team will develop core elements, but local teams will add local adaptations and implement the solution	• Project manager from user liaison organization • U.S. development team • Local implementation team
8	Architecture	Different technology solutions are used around the globe to accommodate differences in infra-structure, vendor support, culture, etc.	Rollout strategy is dependent on the specific IT project	Project team structure is dependent on the specific IT project
9	Architecture	Centralized voice, data, and mainframe operations	Rollout strategy is dependent on the specific IT project	Project team structure is dependent on the specific IT project
10	Enterprisewide	Oracle Financials package	Solution was implemented in North American locations first. Migration is based on business need rather than mandate	• 16 full-time people (half IT, half represent all business areas of the company) • 4-5 Oracle consultants
11	Enterprisewide	Packaged solutions with custom-developed interfaces; AS/400 platform	After a successful pilot, the solution is being rolled out to the rest of the firm	3-tier project structure: • Enterprise policy council (chaired by COO, includes more than 5 other members)—mission to identify mandated, common business processes • Project steering committee (4 people) • Core team (some full-time, includes business representatives who worked on it part-time)

The Deployment of Global IT Solutions

Having examined the nature of global IT solutions, the second broad research question we considered was this: What are successful practices for deploying global IT solutions? We were particularly interested in issues related to development, implementation, and maintenance of the solution, as well as issues related to controlling and coordinating the deployment process. We found that global projects—more so than domestic ones—encompass a set of cultural, physical, structural, and technological boundaries. To be successful, project stakeholders must deal with challenges that arise as they try to cross the boundaries. For example, culturally based differences about speaking out in meetings can, if not fully understood, lead developers to believe that all user needs have been elicited from the group when in fact some participants may not be used to speaking in that forum. Physical boundaries between countries include laws and regulations about transactions; failure to recognize and address such legal issues can result in system errors.

Crossing these boundaries represents significant challenges for the project stakeholders. Based on our research, we have identified a number of strategies and techniques for dealing with these challenges. In some cases, these strategies and techniques will enable the differences to be overcome, in some cases, solution deployment must conform to rules or regulations that cannot be changed, in other cases, managers and individuals on the team must be flexible and adapt to the differences. The goal here is ultimately to help project team members and management learn to *act globally,* which requires a knowledge base of the kinds of boundaries and problems those boundaries cause in solution deployment, as well as a repertoire of ways to address problems. Acting globally means that an individual involved in global IT solution deployment is able to see the types and nature of boundaries that exist, predict the problems those boundaries will cause, and respond appropriately to prevent or minimize the problems.

The strategies and techniques for dealing with the challenges can be classified according to one of four themes: change management, control and coordination, knowledge management, and design choices. In the next four chapters, we discuss the specific cultural, physical, structural, and technological boundaries that project stakeholders must cross and offer strategies and techniques for addressing the challenges that arise. The general framework for presenting this information is shown in Table 10 and will be used in Chapters 4–7.

Table 10. Framework of Strategies and Techniques for Crossing Boundaries

	THEMES			
Boundaries	**Change Management**	**Control & Coordination**	**Knowledge Management**	**Design Choices**
Cultural				
Physical				
Structural				
Technological				

Endnote
[1]See a description of the MSAS Cargo International solution in Ives and Jarvenpaa (1994). More information can also be found at URLs http://www.msas.com and http://www.msas.com/unitel.html.

CHAPTER 4

CROSSING CULTURAL BOUNDARIES

Cultural boundaries arise from differences in norms, attitudes, and behaviors that develop over time in a particular work group or setting. Because the deployment of global IT solutions involves individuals from different work settings, cultural boundaries are evident.

From this study, two such boundaries are identified: readiness for change and communication and decision making. The issues stemming from these two boundaries suggest a number of strategies and techniques for change management, control and coordination, and knowledge management, as depicted in Table 11.

Boundary 1: Cultural Differences in Readiness for Change

Cultural differences between companies in terms of readiness for change can develop from the business environment. These differences have implications for managing change. For example, in the Enterprise Case (I), the company was is in financial crisis and as a result "the employees have embraced the need to change and the degree of support for IT as the vehicle for that change." This enhanced the company's traditionally good general climate for change. In other cases, the cultural differences had a negative effect. For example, in the Production Case (IV. C), some plant managers resisted the global solution because the best manufacturing processes it embodied allowed managers to determine, based on demand from sales data, which production lines should be closed down. Because the full employment of all workers in one country is valued, plant managers from that country were initially hesitant to use this facility.

Table 11. Strategies and Techniques for Crossing Cultural Boundaries

CULTURAL BOUNDARIES	CHANGE MANAGEMENT	CONTROL & COORDINATION	KNOWLEDGE MANAGEMENT	DESIGN CHOICES
Readiness for change	• Leverage existing states of high readiness for change • Sell managers on advantages of new, changed processes			
Communication and decision making		• Ask project team members to adapt communication style • Use low social-presence medium • Provide training on decision making • Ensure that representation for all countries will speak out in meetings • Identify key person to be focal point of control and coordination efforts • Employ control and coordination strategies that are appropriate to all stakeholders	• Select team members with global experience • Provide training in differences in communication and decision making	

Strategies and Techniques for Change Management
- Leverage states of high readiness for change. Organizations where employees are ready for change present an opportunity for large-scale change. This may be the time to make big transformational changes (Enterprise Case).
- Sell managers on the idea that the new changed processes are best processes and that managing according to best practices will advance their careers (Production IV. C).

Boundary 2: Cultural Differences in Communication and Decision Making

There are differences in communication and decision making among individuals from different cultures that can create difficulties related to control and coordination of the project. For example, with respect to differences in communication, users and developers from some countries are often less willing to offer ideas, say no, or ask questions openly in a group (Credit Case IV. H), making it difficult to precisely monitor project progress and to coordinate tasks. Effective control and coordination are also based on trust between parties, and open and honest communication is essential. However, employees from some countries may also be reluctant to notify managers about problems, preferring instead to try to work it out themselves via working harder and more—"add another hour to a twenty-four hour day" (Credit Case IV. H). Businesspeople from some countries expect meetings to begin with about 10 minutes of discussing families, sharing family pictures, and inquiring about family members (Production Case IV. F).

Decision-making differences also lead to control and coordination difficulties, as well as knowledge management challenges. While a U.S. project manager may adopt an "autocratic" decision-making style to maintain progress on the project, this approach may be unacceptable to Asian team members, whose culture demands decision making by consensus (Enterprise Case IV. E). Moreover, the organizational level of the decision maker and the formality of the process vary across cultures. In Japan, for example, there was resistance when the global IT solution empowered decision making at lower levels of management (Enterprise Case IV. B). In Europe, communication is more formal (e.g., in Germany people are not addressed using first names), and decision making must respect the existing hierarchies (Enterprise Case IV. E).

Strategies and Techniques for Control and Coordination
- Encourage all team members to adapt their communications style as needed to conform to cultural norms. Some of these cultural differences require only a small amount of adaptation (being careful about forms of address, conduct meetings in a culturally appropriate way). This adaptation will positively impact control and coordination efforts since it will facilitate the exchange of accurate information among project stakeholders.
- Consider the use of a low social-presence medium such as e-mail when communicating with team members who are reluctant to speak in public a means of communicating (Metrics Case IV. C, H, I).
- To distribute control and coordination activities, give developers who have not had this experience and whose culture tends to centralize control and coordination more decision-making power and training in how to use it (Metrics Case IV. C, H).
- In high interaction meetings, consider representing some stakeholders with individuals from cultures comfortable with speaking out in large groups (Metrics Case IV. B).

- Identify one or a few key individuals in each site, and make a conscious effort to build communication and trust with that person or those persons or cohort(s). Then that person(s) or cohort(s) becomes the translator for other employees (Production Case IV. B). This will enhance control and coordination efforts as it provides a mechanism for open and accurate dialogue.
- Make a conscious determination of the control and coordination strategies to be used in the project that is comfortable for all stakeholders. For example, in the Credit Case, specifications based on input from all locations are distributed back out to all locations for approval. While this step is time consuming, it serves to build consensus and to allow for approvals at all levels necessary. Another example concerns soliciting input from all stakeholders. Prior to a meeting, a project manager may try to forge consensus of Asian stakeholders, while asking U.S. members to contribute individual ideas to an electronic forum, while being sure to coordinate with the appropriate members of the hierarchy in Europe. In the meeting, the manager can then represent the ideas of those who do not voice them, and after the meeting, the manager can revisit the decision with those consulted beforehand.

As shown in Table 11, differences in communication and decision making also impact knowledge management in terms of employee selection and training. Individuals who have experience working cross-culturally are likely to be more effective than those without such experience. Regardless of the level of experience, though, explicit training on cultural differences and on developing appropriate control and coordination strategies would enhance individual effectiveness. However, this type of training is rarely available to project team members.

Strategies and Techniques for Knowledge Management
- Select team members who have experience working and/or living in multiple countries (Credit Case IV. I; Metrics Case IV. B).
- Train team members in cultural differences in communication and decision making at the beginning of the project (Enterprise Case IV. E., F).

CHAPTER 5

CROSSING PHYSICAL BOUNDARIES

The deployment of global IT solutions means that real, physical boundaries will be crossed. These boundaries stem from tangible differences between locations, such as differences in language, currency, and time zone.

This section describes five physical boundaries uncovered in this study: historical hatreds between countries, laws and work regulations, language and currency, time and place, and technology infrastructure. The issues arising from crossing these boundaries relate to control and coordination, knowledge management, and design choices, as shown in Table 12.

Boundary 1: Historical Hatreds between Countries

When the development of the system requires the cooperation of developers and/or users from different countries, the historical relationships between those countries can come into play. Often these poor relationships are between countries that are close geographically and so have been on opposite sides in ongoing conflict and wars. The impact on the global project can be significant. In one case, for example, European managers were unwilling to meet to discuss system needs (Shipments Case, IV. A). This unwillingness to work together directly impacts control and coordination efforts because it is extremely difficult to motivate these managers to work together and to coordinate their tasks to ensure that one common solution is developed.

TABLE 12. Strategies and Techniques for Crossing Physical Boundaries

PHYSICAL BOUNDARIES	CHANGE MANAGEMENT	CONTROL & COORDINATION	KNOWLEDGE MANAGEMENT	DESIGN CHOICES
Historical hatreds between countries		• Build working relationships between managers from those countries		• Accommodate differences in solution design
Laws and work regulations			• Study the local regulations • Use local project team members	
Language and currency			• Select multilingual team members • Use local trainers who are multilingual • Partner with training companies who will translate materials • Establish documentation coordinator position	• Develop a single-language solution • Purchase a multilanguage, multicurrency packaged solution

Time and place		• Provide multiple media for communicating • Hold a kickoff meeting • Utilize established formal liaison roles • Co-locate team members • Select team members who have worked together before	• Develop a strategy for collecting and distributing information • Distribute project documentation to all locations	
Technology infrastructure		• Subcontract to central development team • Maintain competitive salaries • Select team members who are likely to stay • Prevent burnout		

Strategies and Techniques for Control and Coordination
- Encourage the project champion or senior management to try to build a working relationship among the managers from different countries. In the Shipments Case, this working relationship was forged by forcing managers to attend meetings and by encouraging them to socialize.

As noted in Table 12, these historical hatreds can also impact the design choices made. For example, historical hatreds between Korea and Japan led to an unwillingness on the part of the project participants to build network linkages between those two countries (Firm 5, described in Chapter 3).

Strategies and Techniques for Design Choices
- Build network links to avoid connections between certain countries. In the example just cited, the network link for Korea was made to the Netherlands instead of to Japan.

Boundary 2: Legal Differences in Work Rules and Regulations

There are differences among countries in laws and work regulations that must be addressed in the development of the global IT solution. For example, in Europe it is legal to pay a third party or distributors when they help a company get business; the payment is seen as a commission. In contrast, in the United States, such commissions are illegal if they are not made known to the customer (Enterprise Case IV. E). Knowledge management can help mitigate these differences. In particular, an understanding of the local legal and regulatory environments is crucial. Moreover, selecting individuals who have this understanding will enhance the effectiveness of the team.

Strategies and Techniques for Knowledge Management
- Study the laws and work regulations of the local environment.
- Use local project team members who are knowledgeable as to the local legal and regulatory environments.

Boundary 3: Language and Currency Differences

Differences in language and currency contribute to challenges in knowledge management and design (see Table 12). With respect to the former, these types of differences mean that special attention must be paid to selection of team members, training, and documentation. Multilingual team members will be able to bridge many language differences, especially those related to training and documentation. Even in cases where the solution itself is written in English, explaining how to use that solution may require the ability to speak the user's native language (Credit Case III. B), and even solutions such as SAP R/3 that are designed for a multilingual world do not have all training materials and documentation in all languages (Enterprise Case IV. D, E).

Strategies and Techniques for Knowledge Management
- Select team members who know multiple languages or are willing to learn other languages (Enterprise Case IV. E).
- Use a "train-the-trainers" approach to training, where the local trainers speak both the language of the development team and the central training group and the language of the users they are training (Credit Case III. B).
- Partner with computer-based training companies to translate training materials into all languages needed (Enterprise Case III. C).
- Establish a coordinator for documentation who is responsible for all necessary translations of written materials (Enterprise Case).

Design choices are also impacted by differences in languages and currencies across regions. When a solution is to be used globally, the language or languages of the solution must be determined. Organizations must assess the costs and benefits of a one-language solution versus a solution such as SAP R/3 that supports differences in language, currency, units of measure, and so on.

Strategies and Techniques for Design Choices
- Develop the solution for one language, most often English (Credit Case; Shipments Case).
- Purchase a packaged solution that supports multiple languages, currencies, and units of measurement (Enterprise Case II. C).

Boundary 4: Time and Place Differences

There are a great number of time and place differences that might be observed with global projects, as suggested by Table 12. Stakeholders in the project represent many different geographical regions and business units and may not be located at any of the development sites. Project team leadership and members may be distributed across many locations. While there is a need to keep stakeholders and project team members involved in the project, there are not many hours in the day when team members can communicate in "real time" (Shipments Case IV. D). This boundary that arises from time and place differences, therefore, has direct implications for the control and coordination of the project. Motivating individual team members, ensuring that all team members are working on the appropriate tasks, monitoring project progress, and coordinating individual efforts take an enormous effort when project stakeholders and team members are spread across the globe.

Strategies and Techniques for Control and Coordination

- Provide multiple media for communication and information sharing, although in all cases a face-to-face approach was considered essential and the best. Several approaches were used to enable communication across time and place, including travel, telephone, and e-mail (all cases), as well as regular conference calls (Shipments Case IV. C), teleconferencing (Enterprise Case IV. C), and Lotus Notes (Credit Case IV. C).
- Establish intrateam communication initially through a kickoff meeting for the global team (Enterprise IV. C; Shipments Case IV. C).
- Use established formal liaison roles to coordinate project work and communicate (Shipments Case IV. C). This is particularly useful when the individuals in these established liaison roles have personal relationships with key players and in-depth knowledge of the business.
- Wherever possible, co-locate team members, even if for only part of the project term. This helps make interactions more frequent and informal and helps with building team cohesion (Enterprise Case IV. C; Shipments Case IV. C). It is easier to monitor project progress and coordinate individual tasks when team members are co-located.
- Wherever possible, select team members who have worked together before. While formal methods of control and coordination are essential, the informal approaches (such as personal relationships) are also important mechanisms of maintaining project progress. These informal approaches are "the grease and the lubricant that make it all work smoothly" (Shipments Case, IV. C; Metrics Case IV. A).

As shown in Table 12, differences in time and space also lead to knowledge management issues. When project team members are distributed across several locations, it is important that all relevant knowledge be distributed to the appropriate individuals in a timely manner, accurately and completely. However, maintaining and communicating knowledge in this distributed environment is challenging. In addition to the logistics issues presented, the amount of information in these typically large projects can be overwhelming. In some cases (Credit Case IV. C; Enterprise Case IV. E), project team members became overloaded with phone and e-mail messages.

Strategies and Techniques for Knowledge Management

- Develop a strategy for collecting and distributing project-related information over the life of the project (Metrics Case III. A).
- Distribute project documentation during the project to all locations (Shipments Case IV. C).

Boundary 5: Physical Differences in Technology Infrastructure

The final physical boundary noted in Table 12 is that there are differences between and among countries and regions in the technology infrastructure available to deploy and maintain global IT solutions. One aspect of the physical differences is how new technologies are diffused. The pattern that was observed was that a technology that is new and available in the United States will be generally available in Europe in six to twelve months and in Asia in another eighteen to twenty-four months. This means that solutions that employ bleeding-edge technology may not find local vendors or expertise worldwide (Credit Case IV. G).

A second instance of these differences is the availability of technical expertise, which is not available in all locations. In order to deploy global IT solutions that require specialized technical skill, companies have to be able to find or train for necessary expertise, retain employees with skills in a competitive job market, and prevent burnout in key employees. Even when much of the deployment of a global IT solution is centralized, there is need for local expertise for support (e.g., Production Case). When a solution with a central core of functionality that requires local adaptation and implementation (e.g., Shipments Case III. A) is designed, there is even greater need for local developers. Retention of project personnel is difficult when work on the project builds expertise that is rare in some locales (Credit Case IV. D, F). Global IT solutions tend to require large and complex projects, and when project schedules are aggressive, burnout of key project personnel in some locations can cause problems (Enterprise Case IV. D). Obtaining and retaining effective personnel in all locations is a difficult deployment issue.

Strategies and Techniques for Control and Coordination
- When local expertise is not available and local development is expected, then local adaptation work can be subcontracted back to the central development team (Shipments Case IV. B).
- Keep salary competitive in order to retain expert employees, even when that means resorting to techniques such as giving individuals VP titles (Credit Case IV. D).
- When work on a project is likely to develop highly valued expertise in project team members, select team members who are less likely to change jobs (e.g., because of family ties to an area) (Enterprise Case IV. D).
- Help developers develop and use self-care techniques (e.g., relaxation techniques) that prevent burnout (Enterprise Case IV. D).

CHAPTER 6

CROSSING STRUCTURAL BOUNDARIES

Differences between organizational functions and between hierarchical levels of an organization give rise to structural boundaries. For example, a boundary may exist between an IS unit and a manufacturing unit within an organization. Or differences in status between a senior manager and a clerical employee may give rise to a structural boundary.

Table 13 identifies the five boundaries in this research: business processes, business priorities, scope and nature of change from the global IT solution, the lack of existing global coordination mechanisms, and data quality. In addition, techniques and strategies for dealing with issues related to change management, control and coordination, knowledge management, and design choices are included in Table 13.

Boundary 1: Differences in Business Processes

Often there is a history of very independent operations being encouraged or tolerated in different countries or regions. There are many reasons that a business process may differ across business units. Units for once-separate companies may be added to the organization through mergers and acquisition. In the Enterprise Case (II. C), some subsidiaries had been recently acquired and were still using their existing unique systems. Units may have been urged to innovate and develop their own unique processes that are closely tailored to the specifics of their environment. For example, the company in the Shipments Case (I) had regions that had always been "very self-sufficient, isolated," and their processes and systems reflected that. In the Enterprise Case (II. A), functional areas rather than a global supply chain had historically been the focus of operations. Sometimes differences are underestimated when business managers fail to see that the global solution deployment requires or is an opportunity for reengineering business processes but see it as merely a technology problem and solution (Credit Case II. B., IV. A).

Table 13. Strategies and Techniques for Crossing Structural Boundaries

STRUCTURAL BOUNDARIES	CHANGE MANAGEMENT	CONTROL & COORDINATION	KNOWLEDGE MANAGEMENT	DESIGN CHOICES
Business processes	• Allow enough time to build consensus on common business processes • Get and communicate top management support • Build consensus through meetings • Build consensus through one-on-one negotiations • Mandate common business processes • Highlight problems with independent operations and systems • Argue the advantages of common processes • Make change in increments	• Encourage many developers to travel to many sites • Arrange meetings with representatives of sites • Select project team members with business background • Assign a liaison to go between users and IS • Assign specific responsibility for processes and data • Reward managers' cooperation • Meet deadlines to maintain buy in • Build expectation for continuous process improvement • Create local champions of consistency	• Train workers in new, common (and perhaps expanded) business processes • Involve Human Resources Department in job analysis and preparation of employees	
Business priorities	• Create commitment through change management meetings	• Assign extra help to locales when the global IT solution is low priority for local management • "War council" to explain priority		
Scope and nature of change from global IT solution				• Implement first where change scope is lowest; implement last in locations with highest change scope
Few or no existing global coordination mechanisms		• Identify an existing group or team to control and coordinate work • Use project manager as conduit for coordination information • Create a new team to coordinate implementation		
Data quality		• Assign responsibility for data quality in each locale • Expect core project team to help clean data		

The existence of such differences in business process presents a challenge to manage the change to a new, common global IT solution. For example, in the Shipments Case (I. A), there was a history of building separate solutions for each country or region. In the Production Case (IV. C), manufacturing plant managers had their own systems that supported the unique manufacturing processes employed at each plant. Overcoming this history of local processes and systems requires significant change management. The change management issues that occur with all *new* solutions are exacerbated when the solutions is also global.

Strategies and Techniques for Change Management
- Realize that building consensus on the business processes for the global solution will take considerable time before the actual start of the project as well as throughout deployment (Credit Case II. B, IV. A, B).
- Get top management support for the common business processes and solution, and have management communicate that support publicly. In the Enterprise Case (IV. A), the senior management wrote a letter stating that the global solution was the prime initiative for the company. This was used by project team managers with local managers in forging consensus and getting cooperation.
- Use meetings with stakeholders (business representatives from divisions and regions, as well as technology representatives) to negotiate and build a consensus for a common business process and solution (Credit Case II. B; Enterprise Case IV. B; Metrics Case III. A).
- Use one-on-one negotiations between IS and functional area managers from the countries/regions (Shipments Case, IV. E; Credit Case III. B).
- Senior business managers can mandate common business processes and standard ways of operating (Shipments Case, IV. A) and can require that all reports come from the common solution (Production Case IV. C).
- Highlight the information problems with existing, independent applications (Metrics Case II. B). In the Production Case (IV. A), the project manager had a diagram of the company's information flows (that looked like spaghetti) to compare to the flows with the new global solution. In the Credit Case (II. B), the project team documented all existing systems' strengths and weaknesses, identified areas for improvement, and compared those to a functional specification and cost estimate for a global solution. In both cases, this detailed comparison of the current situation with the future state using the global solution helped build the identified need for commonality.
- Argue that the common solution will enable consolidation of operations in separate countries where tax incentives (e.g., from the European Union) encourage combinations (Enterprise Case II. C).
- During the project, use an incremental development strategy so that change is made in increments (Shipments Case III. A). This means that if there is personnel turnover, there are small pieces of the solution to reassess and negotiate if that is needed (Credit Case IV. D; Enterprise Case IV. D).

Overcoming the structural differences in business processes also requires significant control and coordination effort, as noted in Table 13. Three main areas of effort are (1) the initial gathering of input from all units about their needs, (2) assigning and rewarding formal responsibility for common processes, and (3) maintaining commonality over time. First, it is critical that input from all users be obtained in order to have a successful solution. As in any solution, developers have to know about user requirements in order to build a system or adapt a package. In global IT solutions, developers will also have to derive the common processes and data. It is equally important to communicate, via the visibility of getting user input for all locations, that the solution is truly global, not a single-site solution rolled out around the world. Second, formally assigning a specific person or group the responsibility for common processes and data provides incentive for this effort. Third, it may be especially difficult to maintain consensus over time because there is little personnel continuity, both in the business units (the managers who "bought in" to the global solution) and in the project team. The personnel who were involved in forging the original consensus remember the spirit of the agreements as well as the discussions that support them (Credit Case IV. D). This is a problem both during the project deployment (Production Case IV. D) and afterward during maintenance.

Strategies and Techniques for Control and Coordination
- Developers can travel to many/all sites to gather information about existing systems and processes (Credit Case II. B; Enterprise Case III. A).
- Another approach is to gather user representatives from most/all sites and have them discuss and define requirements in several-day meetings (Metrics Case III. A., IV. B). In this case, there were actually two such meetings with communication continuing during the two-month interval between them via e-mail.
- Project team members who are from the various business areas and those who are business-IT hybrids with both types of experience are invaluable for their understanding of the business perspective (Enterprise Case II. B).
- Communicating user requirements to developers may require a liaison who travels to get face-to-face communication with both users and developers (Credit Case IV. A). For example, in the Metrics Case (II. C), the business program manager, who was responsible for the user specifications, communicated with the users via meetings and e-mail, and twice traveled to the development site, once to understand the developers' need for more granular information and a second time to resolve developers' issues with the user specifications.
- It is also possible to have members of the development team assigned responsibility for specific data or work processes; in that case each developer had to deal with a specific constituency (Production Case II. C; Enterprise Case II. B). This representative may in fact be hired by the constituency as was the European user representative in the Shipments Case (II. C).
- Link success of common global IT solution to managers' bonuses and performance appraisals (Production Case IV. B).
- Meet implementation deadlines to maintain buy in (Enterprise III. B).
- Senior managers can build an expectation that the processes in the solution will be continuously revisited and improved over time so that any future problems with the common processes are already planned for later resolution (Enterprise IV. A).
- Local business management should be encouraged to be "champions of consistency," since they will enforce use of the system and prevent local adaptation (Production Case IV. G).

Common global IT solutions that change the way business processes are performed in some or all locations may significantly expand the jobs of some workers, which has implications for managing a firm's knowledge base. For example, some workers will need to think of transactions as a companywide (or even intercompany) process, not as just what part of the transaction their unit performs (Production Case IV. C). In the Enterprise Case (IV. B), the new system enabled some order entry workers to expand their responsibility to evaluating customer credit, but many resisted this job expansion. When this impact of the solution on the nature of work is not expected, it can lead to resistance (Enterprise Case) and/or high turnover (Production Case, II. D., IV. D).

Strategies and Techniques for Knowledge Management
- Prepare workers for possible change through training that goes beyond use of the technology to a conceptual understanding of how work processes will be changed globally (Enterprise Case III. C). This was not done in the Production Case (IV. C), and this was identified as a major cause of high turnover after solution implementation.
- Involve the human resources department in projects that are likely to significantly impact job design so that this type of impact on jobs can be prepared for in better ways (Enterprise Case IV. B).

Boundary 2: Differences in Business Priorities

It is not unusual to find that managers in different locations and functional areas assign a different priority level to the implementation of a global IT solution. This variation may stem from differences in need or readiness for change (discussed earlier). When local management makes it clear that the project has low priority for them, this commitment disjoint can result in missed deadlines (since no one locally cares) (Production Case IV. E). This problem has the most impact when the project requires more local work on data cleaning, development, or implementation.

In this research, the structural differences in business priorities were addressed by one change management strategy and two control and coordination techniques, as articulated here.

Strategy for Change Management
- In order to raise the priority for the solution locally, change management meetings well in advance of implementation in each locale were used in the Enterprise Case (III. B., IV. B) and in the Credit Case (III. B). During these meetings, a contract (implicit or explicit) was agreed to between the area implementation team, the local management, and solution sponsors.

Strategies and Techniques for Control and Coordination
- Successful implementation in some locales where the project is viewed as low priority may change project work assignments to other than local management. In the Production Case (IV. E), middle managers at some locations and the central project team did "double work" to get the solution deployed.
- In one case a "war council" was required to enforce the agreement created in the change management meeting about solution priority. In the war council, senior managers and process managers met with local management to communicate the mandate for the new global IT solution (Enterprise Case IV. B).

Boundary 3: Differences in Nature or Scope of Change

The scope of change created by the global IT solution will vary across locations. One aspect of this scope difference has to do with the existing state of systems and data in the locale. For example, a business unit or region that already has many satisfactory systems in place may be reluctant to replace them with the common solution/processes, especially if those common solution/processes are viewed as less powerful than what is already in place (Credit Case III. B, IV. F; Metrics Case IV. C, D). In this study, the main impact of structural differences in the scope of change was on the design choices for the solution, as shown in Table 13.

Strategies and Techniques for Design Choices
- Implement the system first in locations with few existing systems (low scope of change) and last in the locations that will experience the highest scope of change since they already have well-developed systems and procedures (Credit Case III. B; Metrics IV. C).

Boundary 4: Few or No Coordinating Mechanisms for Global Action

Implementation of systems on a global scale requires some kind of mechanism for coordination and control of effort on a global basis (Credit Case III. B, IV. E). Sometimes it is hard to know ultimately who is responsible for what on the project (Shipments Case IV. F). In this study, some companies addressed the need for global cooperation by expanding the role of existing employees or groups, especially the project manager, and some created new coordinating mechanisms.

Strategies and Techniques for Control and Coordination
- Identify a standing group or position as one that, for this project, will serve a central coordination role. For example, in the Credit Case (IV. C, E), the Analysis/Quality Assurance group served as a major coordination vehicle.
- The project manager can also serve as a conduit between the multiple project subteams as well as the multiple, distributed constituencies. This is perhaps most evident when several people are seen as the project manager, as in the Metrics Case (IV. A), and so this coordination role fell as an extra, unassigned responsibility to the person who served on several subteams.
- In two cases the project management created a new type of team for implementation across locations. This team serves as a partner with each location in the implementation. In the Enterprise Case (II. B, III. B) and the Credit Case (III. B), area implementation teams were created to implement the solution in all sites within their regions. This team was responsible for preparing sites for change, holding change management meetings prior to implementation, and on-site work during implementation.

Boundary 5: Differences in Data Quality

Finally, as shown in Table 13, there are differences between business units and areas in existing data quality as well as in adherence to data standards. For example, the inability to convert data to the new system (because of poor data quality) caused a major delay in implementing the production (II. D) solution in one site. Preparation for the conversion of existing data into a solution such as SAP R/3 involves considerable data cleaning (Enterprise Case II. B, III. B).

Strategies and Techniques for Control and Coordination
- Identify responsibility for data quality in each locale well in advance of the planned rollout. This role may be shared between the project staff and the locale (Metrics Case III. B) or done completely by local IT staff or "power users" (Enterprise Case II. B).
- The core project team should be prepared to step in to clean the data (Enterprise Case III. B; Production Case II. D).

CHAPTER 7

CROSSING TECHNOLOGICAL BOUNDARIES

Technological boundaries arise because, across any one organization, different technologies may have been deployed in the past, and a range of different technologies may be part of the global IT solution. Further, there may be a multitude of methods and processes used to build and implement technology-based solutions. Besides differences within an organization, there are differences in local environments that also create technological boundaries; for example, in some regions of the world, specific technologies may not be available or may not be robust or there may not be local expertise to support those technologies.

In this section, the technological boundaries that stem from having multiple development groups, solution versions, and local adaptations are identified and discussed. Strategies and techniques for dealing with related issues, as well as the boundaries themselves, are shown in Table 14.

Boundary 1: Differences in Methods and Techniques

When multiple development groups are involved in the deployment of a global IT solution (a common situation), it is possible that these groups will use different development processes. If these differences in method are left unresolved, unanticipated conflicts can arise. For example, in the Shipments Case (IV. D), development process differences were not assessed prior to the start of development; as a result, the problems that arose from the differences were handled reactively, after much work had been done. In this situation, there were differences between the U.S. and U.K. development teams about what constitutes a complete analysis and complete design. This led to problems when teams were reviewing the work products of others and ultimately resulted in a separation of tasks among the groups that did not require common understanding. In the same project, there were also differences between the tool used for building client interfaces, due primarily to the size and scope of systems developed in the past by the teams. In the Credit Case (IV. F), the development group in Hong Kong was asked to develop a prototype, but because it was not familiar with prototyping, it instead developed a fully functioning system that reflected the requirements skewed to Asian users. Afterward, development efforts were reassigned to various groups. It is also to be expected that multiple, distributed development groups will experience additional costs for travel, communication, and coordination among the groups (Credit Case IV. A, B, I).

Table 14. Strategies and Techniques for Crossing Technological Boundaries

TECHNICAL BOUNDARIES	CHANGE MANAGEMENT	CONTROL & COORDINATION	KNOWLEDGE MANAGEMENT	DESIGN CHOICES
Differences in methods and techniques		• Meet before project to agree on development method • Use senior management to help resolve conflicts • Expect increased costs	• Transfer knowledge via joint implementation work • Train the trainer • Establish formal training center	
Multiple versions and adaptations		• Limit number of versions available at one time • Add new functionality to newest version only • Minimize local adaptations • Sell local management on need to minimize local bolt ons		

Strategies and Techniques for Control and Coordination
- Prior to development, the development teams should meet to discuss and recognize the differences in how they build solutions, to reach consensus on the exact meaning of development terminology, and to agree on appropriate development processes, tools, and terminology (Checklist III, Development; Metrics Case IV. E).
- Resolution of differences may require senior management intervention at a level high enough to mandate the use of a tool or method (Shipments Case IV. D).
- The increased costs from using multiple, distributed development groups should be anticipated and estimated as part of the costs of deploying the solution (Credit Case IV. F; Metrics Case II. C, IV. A).

Differences in methods and techniques mean that there is a need to transfer the knowledge gained through experience by the multiple development groups, as noted in Table 14. This knowledge should be transferred both between development groups and from development groups to the organization. This knowledge transfer may be done informally (through joint work) or through formal training structures.

Strategies and Techniques for Knowledge Management
- Shared responsibility for implementation between central and local development groups is an excellent mechanism for knowledge transfer (Credit Case III. B; Enterprise Case IV. F, G; Metrics Case III. B; Shipments Case III. C).

- Shared responsibility for implementation between the central team and local team can form the basis for a train-the-trainer strategy, in which knowledge is first transferred to a few key local people who then are responsible for training the others in their locale (Enterprise Case IV. F; Production Case III. B). However, in the Production Case (III. B, IV. C), this train-the-trainers approach was not viewed as a successful approach and, in fact, caused at least to some extent subsequent delays and turnover.
- Establish a formal training function to transfer knowledge from the centralized project team to the area implementation teams (Enterprise Case III. C).

Boundary 2: Multiple Versions and Adaptations

The second boundary shown in Table 14 concerns the development and maintenance of multiple renditions of a global IT solution. The cost of maintaining multiple versions of the solution and any local adaptations to a core system can be high, and the acceptability and responsibility for maintenance needs to be clearly assigned (Shipments Case IV. F). In the Credit Case (III. A, IV. E), there were some difficulties that stemmed from having three distinct versions in use with some new functionality being added to only one version by different development teams. In the Production Case, it took a six-month-long project to upgrade to the newest version of the enterprisewide package. The "bolt ons" not only must be examined for consistency with a new version, but also their functionality must be compared to that of the new version. In one instance, the new version of the core system had the features provided by the bolt on (Production Case III. C). In the Metrics Case (III. C), there is no clear strategy for dealing with long-term support and maintenance, despite the fact that each region has added bolt ons. One IT manager expressed his fears that there is a "whole administrative support headache that nobody really wants to own up to and they want to kind of pretend that it doesn't exist until things start to break."

Strategies and Techniques for Control and Coordination
- Limit the number of versions available and supported at any one time (Credit Case III. A, C.; Shipments Case IV. F).
- Add new functionality to only the most recent version (Production Case III. C; Credit Case III. C).
- Minimize adaptations to the global solution (Enterprise Case III. A; Production Case IV. G; Metrics Case III. C).
- Try to sell local management on the need for minimizing local adaptations, even though these local bolt ons may be easy to add (Production Case IV. G; Metrics Case II. B, III. A).

CHAPTER 8

DEPLOYMENT TIMELINES

Another way to look at the issues in deploying global IT solutions is to consider **when** in the deployment process a strategy or technique might be used or a challenge may arise. The purpose of this chapter is to present what we have learned about successful or necessary managerial actions in a chronological form. While many deployment strategies, techniques, and challenges discussed in this chapter can be found in any systems development project, the actions identified here are those we found to be of particular importance to global IT solution deployment. We use five stages of deployment for our timeline: prehistory of the project, project initiation, project development, project implementation, and project maintenance. After each action, there is a short discussion of the action and references to specific case studies where fuller details of the issue, its context, and action outcomes can be found.

In addition to placing the strategies and techniques along a timeline, we distinguish between two types of actions. First, some strategies and techniques can be proactively used by managers, regardless of the situation or the nature of the global IT solution. We term these types of proactive managerial actions *What You Control.* Second, some actions we identified in the research were more reactive to the setting or the solution. In some cases, the setting or solution presented an opportunity that could be leveraged; in other cases, the context created problems that had to be solved or minimized. We term these types of reactive managerial actions *What Hand You Are Dealt.*

Prehistory of the Project

In Figure 3 we summarize the issues and challenges that can arise during the prehistory of the project. We then discuss these issues and challenges in detail.

Figure 3. Summary of Deployment Issues during Project Prehistory

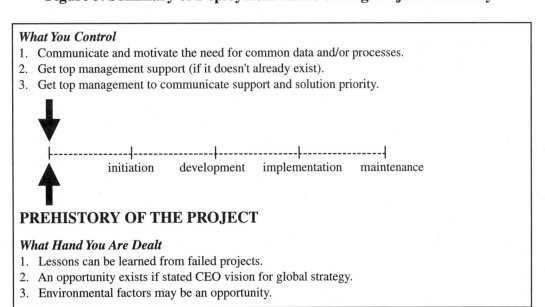

What You Control

1. **Communicate and Motivate the Need for Common Data and/or Processes.** A key to creating motivation for change from a global IT solution is to communicate that there is a real business need for the common data and/or processes that the solution will enable. There may be significant problems in understanding the business because no common data can be reported (Metrics and Production Cases). A symptom of this problem occurs when everyone brings his or her data to a meeting, and the first part of the meeting is used to discuss whose data are correct. There may be a need for common processes in order to present a common face to the customer or to enable easy shifting of personnel between sites or because supporting disparate processes is too costly (Credit, Enterprise, Production, and Shipments Cases).

2. **Get Top Management Support (if it doesn't already exist).** If top management is not the initial sponsor of the global IT solution, then a bottom-up approach to gaining that support must be taken. One way to do this is to have a successful demonstration of the solution in a smaller unit or with a small amount of functionality and showing how the full solution functionality implemented globally would provide even greater benefits (Shipments and Production Cases).

3. **Get Top Management to Communicate Support and Solution Priority.** Management can communicate this support in various ways. The CEO and IT managers can explain the need for the solution and its priority whenever they speak to groups of employees. Brochures, internal house communications, and forums held by leaders at various levels can also be used for communicating this information (Enterprise Case).

What Hand You Are Dealt

1. **Lessons Can Be Learned from Failed Projects.** Previous attempts to build the same or similar solution may have failed. These projects provide important knowledge that can be used in deploying the new and global IT solution (e.g., don't try to build a solution that meets all of everyone's needs; experience in working globally). Employees who participated in these earlier projects should be selected wherever possible for the new project team (Shipments, Enterprise, and Metrics Cases).

2. **An Opportunity Exists if Stated CEO Vision for Global Strategy.** This provides an opportunity to position the global IT solution as an example of enabling that strategy and to help in obtaining top management support (Enterprise Case).

3. **Environmental Factors May Be an Opportunity.** Environmental factors may increase the motivation for change or change of certain types. For example, mergers and acquisitions may provide the push for common data and processes between the newly combined businesses. A financial crisis for the firm may create in employees a high need for change in order to survive (Credit and Enterprise Cases).

Project Initiation

We found that organizations might be faced with numerous challenges and opportunities during project initiation. We summarize these in Figure 4 before discussing them in more depth.

Figure 4. Summary of Deployment Issues during Project Initiation

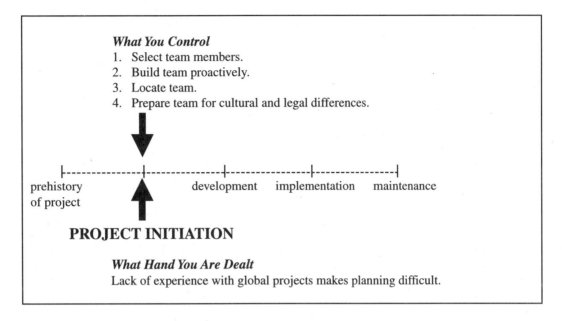

What You Control

1. **Select Team Members.** Where possible, select team members who have multicountry work experience. In some companies, it is common to have employees with a global background and perspective, and these employees will have fewer problems in overcoming boundaries. It is also important to consider individuals who have existing personal relationships with the various stakeholder groups throughout the world since they can leverage those relationships and lines of communication. As one manager noted, "I think personal relationships are the grease and the lubricant that make it all work smoothly" (Metrics and Shipments Cases).

2. **Build Team Proactively.** Given the large scope of most global IT solution projects, the need for extensive travel, and team composition that includes individuals with many differences, there is a great need to proactively build the team. This means the use of the typical kick-off meeting and project logos, social events, and other team spirit–building techniques as well as additional and on-going efforts. Teams need to reconvene at intervals to discuss problems and share lessons learned. For projects with a very large scope/and or an aggressive deadline, managers should provide team members with formal assistance in managing stress, monitor team members for burnout, and encourage individuals to make time for health and relaxation (Enterprise Case).

3. **Locate Team.** Development team location should be considered carefully since the location of teams has costs and other implications. Obviously, the costs of travel and communication between development team sites (for distributed teams) and between user sites should be considered. Other negative outcomes from the selection are possible. Sometime developers resist moves to other countries for the duration of a project, and the supervisors of developers may be reluctant to let employees co-locate (fearing a permanent loss of the employee). Development in one location can lead to solutions that reflect that location, rather than global needs (Credit and Enterprise Cases).

4. Prepare Team for Cultural and Legal Differences. It is possible to prepare employees through training for the important legal differences (e.g., charges that can be detailed on invoices) as well as more subtle cultural differences (e.g., forms of address) that exist in various regions and nations of the world. Sometimes individuals tried to prepare themselves on their own through personal contacts. This is an area in which a formal mechanism for knowledge about such differences is stored and shared.

What Hand You Are Dealt
Lack of Experience with Global Projects Makes Planning Difficult. There are significant money and time costs that global IT solution projects tend to incur. As has been already discussed, there are high travel and communication costs for the developers. There may be costs that are hard to control, such as the cost of license agreements with a state-owned telephone utility that can change significantly when the government changes. There is clearly the time cost of negotiation with various sites over system content and priority, estimated at three to nine months by one project manager. Even after negotiations or agreements are set, there may be further delays. Local managers may signal a low priority for the global IT solution, and this can lead to delays when assigned tasks are not completed (e.g., clean the local data to prepare for conversion to the new global IT solution) (Enterprise and Production Cases).

Developing the Global IT Solution
In Figure 5, we present a summary of the issues and challenges that can occur when the global IT solution is under development. We then describe these issues in more detail.

Figure 5. Summary of Deployment Issues during Development

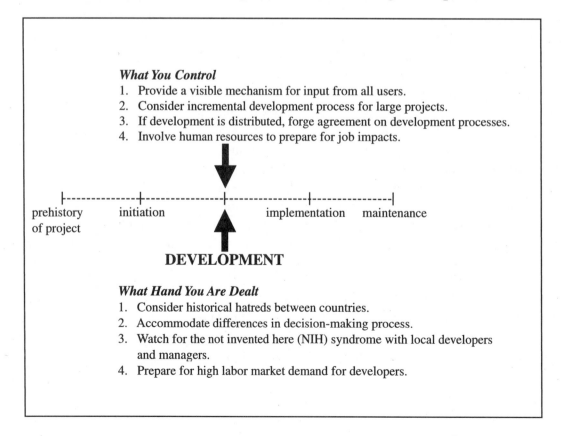

What You Control
1. **Provide a Visible Mechanism for Input from All Users.** This can be done in a variety of ways. Face-to-face meetings with representatives from user groups throughout the world can be used to specify and forge consensus on the data and process requirements for the solution. Ongoing input is possible when a representative of key user constituencies are co-located to the development group. Initial specifications can also be created by having the developers travel to the users' sites to study existing systems and talk with users (Metrics, Shipments, and Credit Cases).
2. **Consider Incremental Development Process for Large Projects.** Incremental development of large global IT solution projects can be advantageous for several reasons. First, when a visible product is produced sooner and at regular intervals, this helps create and maintain support for the project. Increments are smaller and therefore easier to manage, which is important when the global issues are also creating management challenges. The end of each increment becomes a point at which fine-tuning of the development process can be done and the knowledge gained in completing the increment can be formally shared (Enterprise Case).
3. **If Development Is Distributed, Forge Agreement on Development Processes.** There are often differences among development groups as to the tools to be used in development (e.g., tools for building client interfaces) and as to what should be done in systems analysis and design stages. When development is distributed, the various groups of developers will share work on one part of the project, will need to use the work of other groups, or will produce work for other groups. Agreements as to the use of common tools and exactly what they should include, and at what level of detail, in the development of work products should be made (Credit and Shipments Cases).
4. **Involve Human Resources to Prepare for Job Impacts.** Global IT solutions commonly impact the jobs of many users. Often this impact will be job expansion. For example, the solution may provide information that enables an employee to make more decisions, or the use of the system may require as understanding of the entire global business process, not just in his or her small part in the process. This kind of job impact can cause resistance to the solution and/or significant turnover after the implementation of the global IT solution. A tactic to understand job impacts and minimize their negative effects is to include human resource personnel on the project team (Enterprise and Production Cases).

What Hand You Are Dealt
1. **Consider Historical Hatreds between Countries.** While organizations such as the European Union help soften attitudes between and among nations with histories of wars and other conflicts, historical hatreds must still be considered. For example, factors in the selection of regional IT managers often include country of origin and fluency in several languages. In some cases, firms have been reluctant to build network connections that would transmit their data through a rival country. Therefore, it is important that the selection of team membership and management, as well as the design of networks, be informed by an understanding of historical and current relations between and among nations.
2. **Accommodate Differences in Decision-Making Process.** There are real differences between and among groups as to how decisions are made. As discussed in Chapters 4 and 5, cultural and physical boundaries between and among groups are quite real and must be understood and addressed before global IT solution deployment can be effective. In some cultures, organizations tend to be more hierarchical, with decision making done at the top. Other cultures require consensus building with all members of the group prior to decision making. In other groups, the preferred process is based on frank discussions with all conflicts expressed openly. To address these differences, managers need to create situations in which stakeholders or project team members can have a decision-making process that

involves all necessary individuals in appropriate ways. Face-to-face meetings to discuss issues as a group may be the right forum for decision making in one setting; the same kind of decision in another situation may begin with meetings or with e-mails between individuals followed by a meeting to ratify what has been agreed to one-on-one. Realize that decisions made without appropriate processes may be stated, but there may be individuals who are not truly committed to the decision (Enterprise Case).

3. **Watch for Not Invented Here (NIH) Syndrome with Local Developers and Managers.** This is a particular problem when there is a history in the firm of independent, local systems that the global IT solution is to replace. Since the global solution has to meet global needs, it is likely to have features that are not required in all locales and that clearly will not be tailored to one particular location. Local developers and managers need to be prepared for this reality with a global solution and sold on the rationale for the common system. In some situations, the design of the global IT solution allows/requires local adaptation of a core system (Shipments and Production Cases).

4. **Prepare for High Labor Market Demand for Developers**. In some labor markets, it is extremely difficult to find skilled personnel for some project development roles. Realize that work on some global IT solution projects (e.g., SAP) will give individuals rare skills and make retention difficult. Co-location of skilled personnel and training are two ways to deal with the first issue. Retention of skilled developers may require additional salary and titles or be aided by selecting employees for the project who are most likely to stay with the company (Credit, Enterprise, and Shipments Cases).

Implementing the Global IT Solution

We found that a number of challenging issues can arise during the implementation of a global IT solution. We summarize them in Figure 6 and then discuss them in detail.

Figure 6. Summary of Deployment Issues during Project Implementation

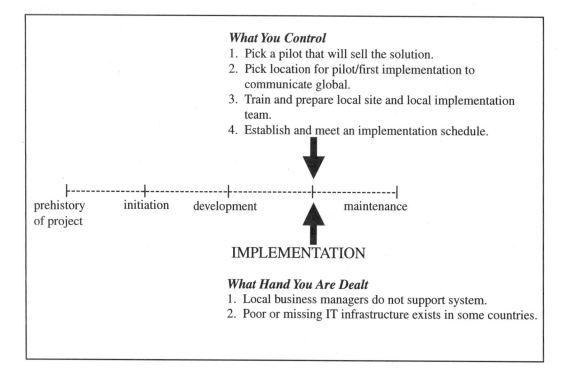

What You Control

1. **Pick a Pilot That Will Sell the Solution.** This tactic is useful in all situations to build and maintain support for the global IT solution and may be critical in situations where the results of the pilot are used to get board approval to fund for the rest of the project. A common approach is to identify a location that has the greatest need for a solution so that local users are ready for change and success is easier to realize. An example of this would be a business unit that has recently been acquired that has completely different systems from the rest of the company. Another approach is to identify a unit that is somewhat isolated and will not be affected by any initial problems (Credit, Metrics and Shipments Cases).

2. **Pick Location for Pilot/First Implementation to Communicate Global.** Besides selling the solution, the location of the pilot/first implementation should not be in the same country as corporate headquarters or the development site. This signals the entire company that this solution will work in the nondomestic units (Shipments, Credit, and Enterprise Cases).

3. **Train and Prepare Local Site and Local Implementation Team.** The transfer of knowledge from the developers to the local implementers and users is a challenge for global IT solutions. Traditional training centers can be used for knowledge transfer between the developer and implementation teams and for users' instruction. One problem is language; even with enterprisewide packages that are designed to be multilingual, the training materials may not be in multiple languages. Translating materials and finding multilingual trainers are challenges and may require a partnership with specialized training companies. A second approach to knowledge transfer is to include developers on the implementation teams at the beginning, with a planned transition away from them as the implementation teams become more knowledgeable. User training can be handled by a train-the-trainer approach; often this choice is driven by the large numbers of users who must be trained. There can be problems in controlling the quality of this kind of training unless curriculum and materials are provided. When designing the training for users, it is important to include two areas of instruction, one to build skill and comfort with the operation of the solution and one to develop an understanding of the global nature of the business process and how the solution supports that process (Credit, Enterprise, and Production Cases).

4. **Establish and Meet an Implementation Schedule.** Consistently meeting an established implementation schedule for a global IT solution signals to the rest of the company that support for full implementation continues. Moreover, locations' realization of the benefits of the solution creates a demand for the system. As described by one project manager, "It's kind of like this is a big freight train; it gets faster every day. So you've got one of two choices: you get on or you get run over. You either will be a part of the process or a victim" (Enterprise Case).

What Hand You Are Dealt

1. **Local Business Managers Do not Support System.** When local management does not set solution implementation as a high priority or provide the resources for that implementation (for example, staff time for data cleaning), then implementation can be significantly delayed. Dealing with this challenge requires upper management intervention. Upper management can mandate the solution either directly or through meetings with the local management and the process sponsors (Production and Enterprise Cases).

2. **Poor or Missing IT Infrastructure in Some Countries.** There are well-known differences between and among countries and regions in the IT and telecommunications infrastructure. This is particularly true with any bleeding-edge technology that may require several years before it is

generally available and supported in most locations. Ways companies can deal with this uneven infrastructure include dealing with vendors on a global basis (rather than selecting vendors in each nation or region), changing system and network design in some areas to reflect infrastructure realities, and building parts of the infrastructure themselves. This last choice may be limited in nations with state-owned telecommunications utilities or extensive regulations on the design and placement of technology.

Maintaining the Global IT Solution

Organizations will face numerous challenges and issues as they maintain and support global IT solutions over time. We summarize these issues in Figure 7 and then discuss them in some depth.

Figure 7. Summary of Deployment Issues during Project Maintenance

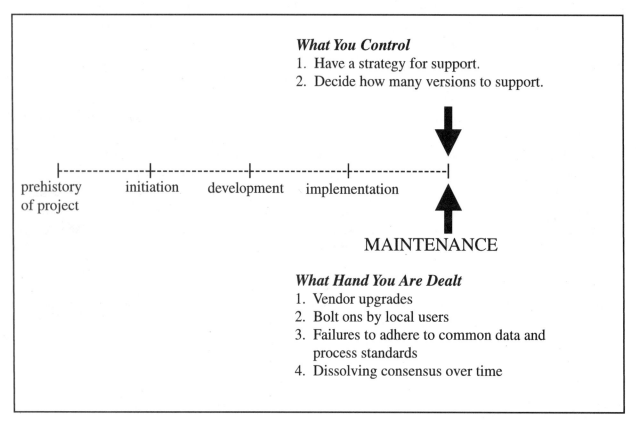

What You Control
1. Have a strategy for support.
2. Decide how many versions to support.

prehistory   initiation   development   implementation
of project

MAINTENANCE

What Hand You Are Dealt
1. Vendor upgrades
2. Bolt ons by local users
3. Failures to adhere to common data and process standards
4. Dissolving consensus over time

What You Control
1. **Have a Strategy for Support.** Support is difficult for global IT solutions because of the differences in skilled personnel availability in all locations, as well as language differences. A common strategy is to provide layered support. The first direct line of support is local and is provided by individuals who speak the users' language and understand the local situation. Problems that cannot be resolved are escalated to higher levels (regional, corporate) where there are individuals with additional skills but who may not be able to communicate directly with the user (Production and Shipments Cases).

2. **Decide How Many Versions to Support.** This is especially difficult when development and implementation are concurrent or when the lack of skilled personnel in some locations makes it unclear that upgraded code will be properly installed and that change control procedures will be followed. The consensus from managers is to minimize versions wherever possible and to have change control procedures in place. One tactic is to create a separate project team to plan, design, and implement each upgrade and to make that team responsible for implementation in locations that have inadequate staff (Credit, Production, and Shipments Cases).

What Hand You Are Dealt

1. **Vendor Upgrades.** When global IT solutions are implementations of enterprisewide packages, vendor upgrades will trigger significant effort. As in the case of upgrades controlled internally, when vendors release an upgrade, a project team should be formed to assess whether or not the upgrade should be implemented and the implications of installing the upgrade (especially if there are local bolt ons that must be maintained separately by the firm) (Production Case).

2. **Bolt Ons by Local Users.** When an enterprisewide package is used for the global IT solution, there may be a legitimate need for bolt ons to the standard system; in fact, packages such as SAP R/3 include authorized exits for these bolt ons. Reasons for such additions include the need to accommodate differences in physical facilities and equipment and/or to add needed functionality. Minimizing these bolt ons is important to minimizing maintenance costs and problems since they must be maintained separately by the firm, and new versions of the package may supersede the bolt on (add the functionality) or cause the bolt on to fail. In some cases, a firm will adopt a "no-modifications" policy to avoid these problems (Production and Enterprise Cases).

3. **Failures to Adhere to Common Data and Process Standards.** Once the global solution is in place, it is possible for local management to develop unauthorized competing or add-on applications or to fail to enforce standards for data quality. One approach to prevent this is to mandate use (e.g., accept reports from the global solution only). It is also important to motivate and reward local managers for being what in one situation are called "champions of consistency." The drive to conformity in the solution should not stifle local innovation, so it is also critical to be open to local suggestions. Someone or a group that maintains the solution should be willing to evaluate local innovations for global implementation: "If it is a good idea, it should be shared and put as an option in all locations, especially since there is a cost to the company to create and maintain such local features" (Production Case).

4. **Dissolving Consensus over Time.** This is a particular problem when personnel turnover means that most or all the individuals who reached the original consensus have left or changed jobs. Even individuals who remain may not remember what was agreed to, what is in the documentation, or the "spirit" of the agreements. This is exacerbated when there is a long time between system requirements specification and implementation. A partial solution to the problem is to build the system in shorter increments although the problem will still exist over the long term. It may be that maintaining consensus is one aspect of a larger issue of how to maintain consistency of global operations in companies, and there is a need for formal *renewal* mechanisms at intervals that are occasions for revisiting these issues (Production Case).

CHAPTER 9
CHECKLISTS FOR DEPLOYING GLOBAL IT SOLUTIONS

This chapter contains a series of checklists intended for project teams who are deploying global IT solutions. The checklists are organized by deployment timeline: preplanning, project initiation, development, implementation, and maintenance. The checklists consist of action items for project managers and team members. The checklists are not meant to be comprehensive but focus on items that are especially relevant because the project is a global one. While no detail is presented in the checklists, there are links to the rest of the book where the issues are discussed in detail. Those links are shown in brackets in the Activity column. The columns labeled Responsibility, Target Dates, and Comments are included as a suggestion as to how the checklist might be used by a project manager but are left blank since the manager of a specific project would complete them.

Stage I: Preplanning Prior to Project Initiation

Activity	Responsibility	Target Dates	Comments
Elicit top management support for the project. [Chapter 6, Crossing Structural Boundaries] [Chapter 8, Prehistory of Project]			
Communicate and motivate the need for common data and/or processes. [Chapter 6, Crossing Structural Boundaries] [Chapter 8, Prehistory of Project]			
Get top management to communicate support and solution priority. [Chapter 8, Prehistory of Project]			
If there have been recent failed attempts to build a global system, examine that project for lessons learned. [Chapter 8, Prehistory of Project]			
If CEO has stated a vision for a global strategy, leverage that statement to build support for the project. [Chapter 8, Prehistory of Project]			
Examine other environmental factors (e.g., a recent merger or acquisition) that might help motivate the project. [Chapter 8, Prehistory of Project]			
Realize that there may be several forces driving the global IT solution, and identify all of them to muster support for the solution. [Chapter 3, What Drives the Deployment of Global IT Solutions?]			

Stage II: Project Initiation

Activity	Responsibility	Target Dates	Comments
Select, wherever possible, team members who have global experience or background and who are multilingual. [Chapter 4, Crossing Cultural Boundaries] [Chapter 5, Crossing Physical Boundaries] [Chapter 8, Project Initiation]			
Select, wherever possible, team members who have experience with previous global projects, even if they were failures. [Chapter 8, Prehistory of Project]			
Select, wherever possible, team members who have worked together before. [Chapter 5, Crossing Physical Boundaries]			
Select, wherever possible, team members with business background. [Chapter 6, Crossing Structural Boundaries]			
Plan and begin team building. [Chapter 8, Project Initiation]			
Select the location for teams with the issues of the costs of communication, travel, and co-location in mind. [Chapter 8, Project Initiation]			
Prepare team members for the cultural and legal differences they are likely to encounter in the project, especially in terms of differences in communication and decision making. [Chapter 4, Crossing Cultural Boundaries] [Chapter 8, Project Initiation]			
Realize that if there is little experience in the firm with global IT solution deployment, planning will be difficult, especially in the area of estimating costs and schedules. [Chapter 8, Project Initiation]			

Stage II: Project Initiation (continued)

Activity	Responsibility	Target Dates	Comments
As desired project outcomes are identified, consider how there may be both *product* and *process* success. [Chapter 3, What Outcomes Are Realized and Anticipated?]			
Identify both tangible and intangible measures of success for the solution. [Chapter 3, What Outcomes Are Realized and Anticipated?]			
Look for differences between locations in readiness for change. [Chapter 4, Crossing Cultural Boundaries]			
Begin building relationships between business managers from various countries. [Chapter 5, Crossing Physical Boundaries]			
Plan for adequate time to build consensus. [Chapter 6, Crossing Structural Boundaries]			
Build consensus through both meetings and one-on-one negotiations. [Chapter 6, Crossing Structural Boundaries]			
Reward managers for cooperation. [Chapter 6, Crossing Structural Boundaries]			
Build an expectation for continuous process improvement. [Chapter 6, Crossing Structural Boundaries]			

Stage III: Development

Activity	Responsibility	Target Dates	Comments
Provide a visible mechanism for input from all users. [Chapter 8, Development]			
Use existing formal liaison roles where possible to help with control and coordination, or create special liaison roles. [Chapter 5, Crossing Physical Boundaries] [Chapter 6, Crossing Structural Boundaries]			
If the project is large, consider an incremental development process. [Chapter 8, Development]			
If development is distributed, forge agreements about the exact meaning and deliverables of development processes and which tools will be used prior to beginning development. [Chapter 7, Crossing Technological Boundaries] [Chapter 8, Development]			
Involve representatives from human resources to prepare users for job impacts from the solution. [Chapter 6, Crossing Structural Boundaries] [Chapter 8, Development]			
Find out if there are historical hatreds between nations that may impact system design or limit communication. [Chapter 8, Development]			
During development, watch for the not invented here (NIH) syndrome in locations not involved in development. [Chapter 8, Development]			
Plan and use tactics, such as higher salaries, to deal with high labor demand in some locations. [Chapter 5, Crossing Physical Boundaries] [Chapter 8, Development]			

Stage III: Development (continued)

Activity	Responsibility	Target Dates	Comments
Try to minimize the number of local bolt-ons allowed, since these are costly during maintenance. [Chapter 7, Crossing Technological Boundaries] [Chapter 8, Maintenance]			
Use communication styles and media that are appropriate to the stakeholders. [Chapter 4, Crossing Cultural Boundaries]			
Use control and coordination strategies that are appropriate to all stakeholders. [Chapter 4, Crossing Cultural Boundaries]			
Identify a key person or group to be the focal point of control and coordination efforts. [Chapter 4, Crossing Cultural Boundaries] [Chapter 6, Crossing Structural Boundaries]			
Study local regulations that may impact the solution. [Chapter 5, Crossing Physical Boundaries]			
Use team members from local sites who will know about local regulations and issues. [Chapter 5, Crossing Physical Boundaries]			
Establish documentation coordinator position to ensure that documents are prepared and translated appropriately. [Chapter 5, Crossing Physical Boundaries]			
To overcome language differences, consider developing a single-language solution or purchasing a multilanguage, multicurrency packaged solution. [Chapter 5, Crossing Physical Boundaries]			

Stage III: Development (continued)

Activity	Responsibility	Target Dates	Comments
Co-locate team members to improve control, coordination, and communication. [Chapter 5, Crossing Physical Boundaries]			
When local teams are expected to do local development and adaptation, realize they may not have the expertise and so may subcontract the task back to the central development team. [Chapter 5, Crossing Physical Boundaries]			
Prevent team member burnout proactively. [Chapter 5, Crossing Physical Boundaries]			
Assign responsibility for data quality and consider who will do the data cleaning work. [Chapter 6, Crossing Structural Boundaries]			

Stage IV: Implementation

Activity	Responsibility	Target Dates	Comments
Pick a pilot location that will sell the solution. [Chapter 8, Implementation]			
Pick a pilot or first implementation that will communicate the global nature of the solution. [Chapter 8, Implementation]			
Implement first in locations where the scope of change is lowest and last in locations with highest scope of change. [Chapter 6, Crossing Structural Boundaries]			
Train and prepare local site managers and users for implementation. This training should include both system use and the new, common, and perhaps expanded business processes. [Chapter 6, Crossing Structural Boundaries] [Chapter 8, Implementation]			
Consider the pros and cons of using formal training centers and/or "train-the-trainer" approaches. [Chapter 7, Crossing Technological Boundaries]			
Sell local managers on the advantages of the new, changed processes. [Chapter 4, Crossing Cultural Boundaries]			
Train the local implementation team; in particular, find a way to transfer knowledge from the development team. [Chapter 7, Crossing Technological Boundaries] [Chapter 8, Implementation]			
Establish and meet an implementation schedule to maintain support for the solution. [Chapter 8, Implementation]			

Stage IV: Implementation (continued)

Activity	Responsibility	Target Dates	Comments
If local business managers do not support the solution, assign extra personnel to help and get their supervisors and other top managers to intervene. [Chapter 6, Crossing Structural Boundaries] [Chapter 8, Implementation]			
If there is poor or missing infrastructure in some countries, then prepare alternative implementation designs or build your own infrastructure. [Chapter 8, Implementation]			
Use local trainers who are multilingual. [Chapter 5, Crossing Physical Boundaries]			
Consider partnering with training companies who will translate materials. [Chapter 5, Crossing Physical Boundaries]			

Stage V: Maintenance

Activity	Responsibility	Target Dates	Comments
Create a strategy for supporting all locations, recognizing the differences in language and support personnel available. Consider a layered structure in which maintenance requests are fielded locally and then escalated up when necessary. [Chapter 8, Maintenance]			
Decide how many versions of the solution to support at any one time. [Chapter 7, Crossing Technological Boundaries] [Chapter 8, Maintenance]			
Add new functionality to latest version only. [Chapter 7, Crossing Technological Boundaries]			
When a package is used, vendor upgrades will create a need for a maintenance project. [Chapter 8, Maintenance]			
When there are maintenance activities, remember to analyze the effect on local bolt-ons. [Chapter 8, Maintenance]			
Monitor whether all locations are adhering to common data and process standards and intervene where needed. [Chapter 8, Maintenance]			
Realize that consensus will dissolve over time, especially if there is high turnover, and exert effort to renew consensus. [Chapter 8, Maintenance]			
Create local "champions of consistency" in local managers. [Chapter 6, Crossing Structural Boundaries]			

CHAPTER 10

LESSONS LEARNED

Today's business environment has been called dynamic and turbulent. Indeed, there is a sense of inconstancy, with the number of mergers, acquisitions, and failures increasing. In part, these changes are due to rapid globalization—the fact that many firms have suppliers, partners, and customers that are global in scope. These changes in the environment have forced many firms to radically adjust their business processes, products, structures, and roles. Information technology is often the catalyst for making these changes. Global IT solutions, in particular, enable or facilitate efforts to transform a firm into one that can compete in the global arena.

In this book, we set out to describe the nature of global IT solutions and best practices for building and implementing these solutions. We found that global IT solutions—whether infrastructure choices, single-function solutions, or cross-functional solutions–span geographic and other boundaries to support global business processes. Firms deploy these solutions for a variety of reasons, but often they do so because the solutions are needed to meet strategic initiatives related to cost reduction or to enable a global business process or product.

With respect to deploying global IT solutions, we found many challenges to attend to. Global project teams, as well as senior IS and business management, must cross cultural, physical, structural, and technological boundaries in order to successfully deploy these solutions. Crossing these boundaries means that issues related to change management, control and coordination, knowledge management, and design choices must be articulated and resolved.

While the previous chapters have described a number of best practices, strategies, and techniques for deploying global IT solutions and have presented deployment timelines and checklists, we would like to conclude by offering lessons learned for the successful deployment of global IT solutions. We have identified four broad lessons about organizational change, the role of business and IT management, technological implications of working on a global project, and project team composition. Each lesson is described here along with specific points related to it.

Lesson 1: Deploying a Global IT Solution Is an Exercise in Organizational Change

One of the clear messages from this study is that the deployment of a global IT solution is all about implementing change. These change efforts are sometimes driven by business managers and sometimes by IS. But in virtually all efforts that we studied, it is not just the technology that is changing; there are also major—and sometimes transformational—changes occurring in the business as well. In the following sections we discuss three points related to managing change in the context of deploying global IT solutions.

Point A: It Takes Vision to Become Global

The deployment of a global IT solution often accompanies a firm's desire to become a global firm. The change to a global firm is not accidental but is part of a firm's strategic initiatives. Implementing global IT solutions can facilitate this change to a global firm, but this is not accidental either. The process requires a champion who will proactively marshal resources and act as an advocate.

Point B: The Firm Must Identify, Build Commitment to, Communicate, and Enforce Common Business Processes, System Priorities, and Appropriate Data Standards

Implementing global IT solutions means that some business processes, systems, and data will be standardized and common across the organization. For those firms for which local units define and control their own processes and data, this move to standardization represents a significant change. The time required identifying standards and negotiating acceptance of common processes and data standards can be significant (months) and should be anticipated in the project schedule.

Point C: Implementing a Global IT Solution Requires a Carrot and a Stick

Virtually all of the firms actively sold the change represented by the global IT solution on a business need or value basis. In addition, incentives such as bonuses, staffing, and other resources were offered to help individual units and employees make the transition to the new environment. However, the message to the firm's employees was also clear: Adapt to the change or leave. So, while carrots were offered, the stick was present as well.

Lesson 2: Both Business and IT Management Must Be Actively Involved in the Deployment of a Global IT Solution

Deploying a global IT solution is not just a technical activity but, as discussed previously, involves changes to organizational processes and activities. There is therefore a need for business and IT management to work together to ensure the successful implementation of the solution. We discuss two specific points next.

Point A: Senior Business and IT Managers Must Act as Change Agents

Because the deployment of global IT solutions involves changes in work processes, a critical role for senior management—both IT and business managers—is to act as change agents. It is important that these mangers motivate the need for change and actively advocate change. Specific training is sometimes needed for change management techniques, including how to think about and lead change. It is important to recognize that individuals deal with change by going through stages, much as they go through stages when faced with other traumas.

Point B: A Critical Role for Senior Management Is to Manage Business and Technological Risks

The source of business risk in projects designed to deploy global IT solutions stems from the difficulty in getting dispersed units to agree on common work processes and data standards and then to actually make the changes required to conform. The technological risks include the nature of the solution (have other firms successfully implemented this software, on this platform, at this scale?) as well as the availability of appropriate infrastructure and technical expertise. One approach is to think about these risks in combination and make trade-offs between them. For example, when there is high business risk, seek a low-risk technical solution.

Lesson 3: Deploying a Global IT Solution Has Technological Implications

Developing a technology-based solution that will be implemented in many countries presents a number of technological challenges. Project team members are no longer developing a specific solution for a specific site, nor are they developing solutions that include both common elements and components that can be tailored for individual sites. Moreover, developers are not just writing code but also taking on more of a systems integrator role in which they bring together and configure different applications, different telecommunications networks, and different hardware platforms. In the following sections, we present and discuss six specific points related to deploying technology on a global scale.

Point A: The Deployment of Global IT Solutions Has the Potential for Large Cost Savings and the Possibility of Significant Hidden Costs

Many firms implement global IT solutions, hoping to reap significant cost savings by eliminating redundant practices, streamlining business processes, and standardizing on fewer systems. These benefits can be realized, but potential, less obvious costs may be incurred. Among the hidden costs are these:

- Building infrastructure, with supporting software and hardware, when no or poor infrastructure exists.
- Additional training and/or fly-in of experts to address the lack of local expertise.
- Additional or different technologies when local work rules or regulations force changes.
- Building and using technologies that are leading/bleeding edge for a specific locale or worldwide.

Point B: A Single Firm Cannot Overcome All Problems From Intercountry Differences

The work rules and government regulations in individual countries, which limit what can be done, by whom, and when, are not likely to be changed by one foreign firm. Instead, firms must find a way to either work around these rules or to partner with other companies with required expertise and experience.

Point C: The Global Infrastructure Is not Robust

There are vast differences around the globe in terms of the robustness of the global infrastructure. In some countries, for example, reliable telecommunications facilities are not available. Because a working global infrastructure cannot be assumed, firms must

- Exclude certain regions from the solution.
- Build their own infrastructure.
- Develop a less technologically sophisticated work around.

Point D: Many Vendors Have Difficulty Delivering Global Products and Services

Not all vendors are licensed to provide products in all countries. In some countries, the local government mandates the only source for some equipment or services (especially in the telecommunications area). In addition, response from local vendors may not be timely or adequate. Firms deploying global IT solutions must secure an appropriate level of vendor service.

Point E: It Is Important to Implement a Global Solution that Supports Multiple Languages and Currencies and That Is Scalable

It is important that project team members be sensitive to differences among countries. Implementing some packaged solutions (e.g., enterprisewide packages such as SAP R/3) can help address some of the intercountry differences such as language and currency. Another difference that arises between locations is size; some sites may be single-user locations while others may have hundreds or thousands of users. This difference in size means that the global IT solution must be scalable. Some technologies, such as client/server, are more easily scaled than others.

Point F: Leading-Edge Technology Choices May not Always Be Appropriate
Technology is constantly changing, and because of the scope and magnitude of the organizational changes accompanying global IT solutions, many firms use this project as an opportunity to install new technology. While this new technology may provide needed functionality, it can result in pains for the project team and lasting scars for the users. This can be particularly problematic for global projects because these projects already encompass so much change. Adding new and unproven technology into the mix might be more than the project team and users can bear.

Lesson 4: Project Team Composition Is a Critical Success Factor for the Deployment of a Global IT Solution

Putting together the "right" project team is essential to the success of the project. The team members must not only have appropriate technical expertise, but also they must understand the business as well as the changes that the firm is undergoing. The team must be able to carry senior management's vision forward and must be able to echo that vision to the users. Team members must understand and communicate what is happening to the organization at the same time that they are involved in a challenging and complex technical project. Selecting project team members who can adapt to the business changes while developing a technical solution is challenging. Moreover, retaining individuals who are acquiring and perfecting very marketable skills is another challenge. We discuss four points related to project teams next.

Point A: Developers Need a Broad Range of Technical Skills Plus a Global Business Perspective
The range of technical skills needed is broad because global solutions usually involve multiple platforms and networks. A global IT solution might not only reside on a different hardware platform and use a different telecommunications network from site to site but also the solution might interface with a different set of applications at each site. Besides needing a broad range of technical skills, project team members need the capability to think and act globally from a business point of view. They must recognize that the solution is meant to satisfy many sites, not a particular location; therefore, the solution itself will be a negotiated compromise among many stakeholders.

Point B: The Composition of Project Teams Is Critical
Because so many different skills are needed to successfully deploy a global IT solution, the composition of the project team must reflect the varied skills. A person who understands the business and the changes that the firm is trying to achieve must lead the team. This person must possess excellent negotiation skills in order to ensure that all relevant needs are incorporated into the final solution. In addition, this person must be credible in the eyes of the project team members and users. Team members who understand the big picture and have local expertise are required. When putting together a team, it is also important to recognize that both global and local business area representations are desired so that the needs of the individual units, as well as common and corporate needs, can be taken into consideration as the global solution is under development. The implementation of a global IT solution represents an

opportunity to communicate the existence of a truly global (versus local) solution. An implementation team with both corporate and local personnel can foster acceptance of both the global IT solution and the changed work processes.

Point C: The Location of the Project Team Impacts the Team's Ability to Effectively Work Together
Co-located team members can improve the team's effectiveness and efficiency. Being in the same location helps bridge differences in culture, norms, and processes, and it helps team members build and maintain a cohesive and effective working relationship. Moreover, co-location will make control and coordination of the process easier because the people developing different pieces of the solution and the solution components themselves will be in one location. Finally, it is important to balance the location of expertise against the need for global and business area representation to gain commitment and help overcome resistance.

Point D: Retaining Project Team Personnel Can Be Problematic
As firms deploy global IT solutions, the project team members are becoming well versed in "hot" technical skills. For example, there is now great demand for people with knowledge of and expertise in enterprisewide solutions such as SAP R/3. With these skills, project team members are very marketable and may be able to easily move to other firms and command larger salaries. Firms can address this problem by implementing specific measures to retain these individuals; such measures include training in desired areas, challenging work assignments, job changes or promotions, and compensation. Some firms can also rely on and leverage individual loyalty and commitment to the firm as a way to help retain key individuals.

Concluding Comments

As evidenced by these *lessons learned* and points about the deployment of global IT solutions, many issues and strategies are the same as those for any information system. The MIS field has understood for many years that IT deployment is organizational change, that both business and IT management must be actively involved in deployment, that deployment involves significant technological challenges and risks, and that getting the right personnel for project teams is critical. Building successful IT solutions will always require business and IT managers who are able to address the many challenges that arise in each of these areas.

The *differences* for global IT solutions are the magnitude and the nature of these challenges. An example of the magnitude of the challenge is that top management must have and communicate a global vision and strength of commitment to make a change to a common solution. This is necessary at the start of and throughout the project to withstand the pressure from local units to remain or become unique in their data or processing. Getting hundreds of locations and thousands of users to cross existing physical, structural, technological, and cultural boundaries to conform to a single way of performing a business process requires a huge ongoing effort. Global IT solutions require not only greater effort but also managers and project team members from both business and IT who mobilize to deploy the solution and confront different challenges. For example, they must understand and accommodate intercountry differences in work rules and regulation. They must acquire technology and technological expertise in locales in which those resources are scarce. In sum, managers and employees at all levels must learn to think and act globally.

APPENDIX A

INTERVIEW PROTOCOLS

In this appendix are the interview protocols used for both the telephone interviews and for the on-site case studies.

Interview Protocol for Telephone Interviews

Telephone Interview of CIO or Senior IS Manager

Part I: Background Information
1. What is your title?
2. How long have you been in your current position?
3. How long have you worked for this company?
4. Can you tell me a little bit about how the company is organized, and where IS fits in? Where is development located?
5. Where do you fit in? What are your roles and responsibilities?

Part II: Description of Global IT Solution & Link to Firm Strategy
1. Please describe the function and purpose of this solution.
2. What was the firm's motivation for developing this solution?
3. Was there a champion for this project? Why do you think this person championed the effort?
4. What approach was taken to the development of this IT solution? Why?
5. What is the current status of this project?
6. When did this project begin? When did it end?
7. How much did the project cost? [in person-hours; dollars; etc.]
8. Have you developed other global IT solutions? Were they successful?
9. How do you know if this project is a success?
10. What special challenges did you face because this was a global (not domestic) solution?
11. What rules-of-thumb did you develop to deal with these challenges?
12. If you were undertaking this type of project again, what would you do differently? the same?

Telephone Interview of Project Participant

Part I: Background Information
1. What is your title?
2. How long have you been in your current position?
3. How long have you worked for this company?
4. How would you describe your roles and responsibilities?

Part II: Description of How Global IT Solution Built & Deployed
1. Please describe the function and purpose of this solution.
2. What is the current status of this project?

3. When did this project begin? When did it end?
4. How much did the project cost? [in person-hours; dollars; etc.]
5. What is the size of this system? [in lines of code; function points; impact to users; etc.]
6. Describe the hardware and software used: platforms for development and for execution.
7. What were your roles and responsibilities on the project?
8. Please describe the composition of the project team: # of people, roles, location.
9. What approach was taken to the development of this IT solution? (methodology?)
10. Is this an approach that you and the team were familiar with, or used before?
11. Did this approach raise any special challenges for you and the team?
12. What (other) special challenges did you face because this was a global (not domestic) solution?
13. What rules-of-thumb did you develop to deal with these challenges?
14. Have you developed other global IT solutions? Were they successful?
15. How do you know if this project is a success?
16. If you were undertaking this type of project again, what would you do differently? the same?

Interview Protocol for Case Studies

Questions were tailored, as appropriate, for individual respondents.
Part I: Background
1. How is your firm organized? The IS department?
2. What is your title? Who do you report to?
3. Please describe the project: what is its function? Is it replacing an existing system?
4. What was the business motivation for this project?
5. What is the current status of the project?
6. What are target and actual start dates? Target and actual budget? Size of project?
7. Do you use a specific methodology to develop IT solutions?
8. Who are the users?
9. Please describe your roles and responsibilities with respect to the project.
10. Why were you chosen for this role?

Part II: Team Issues
1. How is team organized for this project?
2. Where are team members located?
3. To what extent is the user community involved with this project?
4. How would you describe relations between IT and client personnel?
5. How is the liaison function handled? Is this successful?

Part III: Experience with Global IT Solutions
1. Is this the first global IT solution project that you have dealt with?
2. How is this project similar and different from other projects?
3. Do you have experience working with other countries?
4. Can you articulate challenges that arose because the project was global? How were these challenges resolved?

Part IV: Control
  1. Please describe the goals for this project.
  2. Please prioritize these goals. Which one is most important?
  3. How were goals set? Who was involved?
  4. How do you know that the goals were / will be met?
  5. Is it important to you that a particular methodology be used / followed?
  6. Is it important to you that standards are followed?
  7. How do you motivate people to ensure goals are met?
  8. How do you let people know about the project's status?
  9. Please describe the mix of formal and informal techniques used to exercise control.
 10. How has the use of these techniques (and the mix) changed over the course of the project?
 11. To what extent do you monitor individual activities, vs. expect people to self-monitor?
 12. Describe the performance evaluation process.
 13. Have you found any special challenges in motivating people because the project is global?
 14. Who is ultimately responsible for the success of this project?
 15. Who should be responsible?
 16. Is responsibility shared? How so? Is it possible to share responsibility?
 17. How do you measure success?

Part V: Coordination
  1. What kind of mechanisms do you use to coordinate the work on this project?
  2. Do you use technology (email; groupware) to coordinate work?
  3. Please describe the mix of formal (meetings; liaison roles) and informal (walking around) techniques.
  4. How have your efforts to coordinate activities changed over the course of the project?
  5. Have you found any special challenges because the project is global?

Part VI: Change
  1. How much change to [firm] does this global IT solution represent?
  2. How would you characterize the scope of this change? The magnitude? The pace?
  3. How would you characterize the climate of your organization for change?
  4. Is there a formal strategy here for implementing change? Was it followed?
  5. How do you sustain changes over time (i.e., how to institutionalize change)?
  6. Was there are any resistance to implementing the changes? If so, please describe.

APPENDIX B

CASE STUDY DATA

This appendix contains descriptions of five case studies of global IT solutions at five different organizations. The names of the companies, solutions, and other identifying information have been changed or eliminated from these cases in order to comply with the participating companies' requests for confidentiality. The global IT solutions are as follows:

- The **SHIPMENTS** solution: a **custom-developed application** to support processing for import/export shipments globally.
- The **PRODUCTION** solution: implementation of an **enterprisewide package** to manage manufacturing and related processes and controls globally.
- The **ENTERPRISE** solution: an **enterprisewide package** (SAP R/3) that is in the process of being implemented globally.
- The **METRICS** solution: implementation of **data infrastructure** (data warehouse) to enable the use of standardized metrics on product repair.
- The **CREDIT** solution: a **custom-developed application** that supports letters-of-credit processing globally.

Each case study is presented using the following structure:
- **I. Background.** This section of the case study briefly describes the company and project context.
- **II. Solution and Project Description**. This section includes discussions of the project goals and objectives, history, team structure, and anticipated or realized outcomes.
- **III. Deployment Strategies and Techniques**. This section details the development, implementation, and maintenance methods and processes employed for the solution.
- **IV. Challenges and Resolutions**. This section identifies the critical challenges faced in the deployment of the solution and the way they were and/or should have been resolved in the case.

In earlier chapters, references were made to these case studies using the solution name, section Roman numerals, and when appropriate, letters for subheadings within a section. For example, in Chapter 4, there is a reference to "Production Case (IV. B)." This is intended to direct the reader to the Production Solution case study that is included in this appendix and to the second Challenge and Resolution discussed in that case.

The SHIPMENTS Solution

I. Background

The company that is developing the Shipments solution is a multibillion-dollar firm in the shipping and logistics industry. The company's worldwide headquarters are in the United States; in addition, Asian headquarters are in Hong Kong, and European headquarters are in Brussels. This company employs more than 100,000 people worldwide.

The organizational structure at the company is fairly thin. Reporting directly to the CEO are three executive vice-presidents (Legal, Finance, and Worldwide Operations), as well as senior officers for functions such as Finance, Marketing, and Information Technology Services (i.e., the CIO). Directly reporting to the CIO are several vice-presidents; under the vice-presidents are a number of managing directors.

This company has several ongoing strategic initiatives. One is to get closer to the customer, and the company has been successful in deploying information technology to its customers. A second initiative is to reengineer the import/export process. A third strategic initiative is customer service, in particular, how to integrate with the customers to provide personalized service.

From a global perspective, the international regions within the company have historically acted very independently. One managing director describes the regions as "very self-sufficient, isolated." These regions tend to operate from a tactical perspective, focusing on local needs; the successful implementation of global solutions requires the regions to think more strategically and to consider the needs of the company as a whole.

A. Information Technology Services

The IT function at the company has traditionally been centralized, with senior IS management and a large application development staff located in the U.S. headquarters. In addition, there are application development groups in several other regional offices around the United States, as well as smaller groups in other countries. Most application development is done in the United States, but occasionally applications are developed in non–U.S. locations. Recently, the company has decentralized some of the IT functions. In line with this decentralization initiative, more programmers are being deployed throughout the world; the expectation is that increased development and implementation activities will be located outside the United States.

The company is a large IBM mainframe installation, and a heavy user of products such as COBOL and IMS. While the company expects to maintain this mainframe platform for years to come, it has also been incorporating client/server technology into its IT functions. In particular, within the last four years, it has moved to a more distributed platform, using UNIX-based servers (e.g., HP, Sun, RS6000), Sybase, Oracle, C, and C++.

The majority of this company's development efforts are custom-built applications. In the past, IS responded to specific local needs in several countries. If a country asked for automation help (because of the volume of transactions), IS responded. The end result was a series of custom-built applications for different countries. This kind of strategy for deploying systems is no longer possible, given the level of resources available.

The global IT solution studied for this research effort—the Shipments solution—falls under the responsibility of a Managing Director of Import/Export Services. Though Import/Export Services is part of the corporate IS organization, it is located in a regional U.S. office. The Managing Director of Import/Export Services reports directly to the Vice-President of Worldwide Systems, who is located at the corporate headquarters and who reports directly to the CIO. The Managing Director of Import/Export Services has seven direct reports, including the Systems Development Manager. Ten people currently report to the Systems Development Manager, whose group has one responsibility: the development and delivery of the Shipments solution.

II.   Solution and Project Description
A. *The Project: Goals, Objectives, and Drivers*

The Shipments solution is designed to facilitate import and export processing of shipments: "The goal is to develop a new and improved industry standard for conducting Global Trade. This expands . . . into all of the services and revenue related aspects associated with import and export clearance" (project plan, 1997). The end users are the operations employees of this company as well as people employed by government regulatory agencies such as customs agents.

The primary driver for the Shipments solution is cost reduction, resulting from reengineered shipping processes. The anticipated lowered costs of import/export shipping stem from several changes, including a paperless environment; more accurate billing of customers for various services; increased ability to recover payments from delinquent customers; and faster processing of packages.

The cost reduction driver not only refers to lowered costs for conducting the import/export business, but also it means lowered costs for deploying IT solutions. In particular, the company wants the ability to take the software off the shelf and easily integrate it into a new location. Moreover, while that solution will contain "core" and "common" components, it can also be tailored for the needs of the local site. In this scenario, corporate IS is responsible for building the core and common components, while regional sites will add local components and then implement the system.

Another driver is to integrate existing data and systems. In many locations, the end users have up to four computer terminals to access disparate systems. The data are not integrated across those systems. All of these systems, and the old hardware, will be replaced by the Shipments solution, which will provide "the integration, the seamless flow that we want" (project manager).

The official start date for the Shipments solution was June 1996. A preliminary planning document estimates a multiyear, multimillion-dollar effort to complete the overall project. The scope of the project is considered very large and complex within this company. The overall project is broken into increments (see section III for an explanation of "increments"). The start date for increment Number 1 is February 1997; its estimated budget is between $2.5 million and $3 million, and its target implementation date was October 1997.

B. *Project History*

While the project's official start date was 1996, its roots date back to the early 1990s. The Shipments solution is the "brain child" of the European Sponsor. When working in Canada, this person had championed the automation of the Canadian import/export operations; the Shipments solution initiative began as her push to update European operations, beginning with the United Kingdom, which is where the European sponsor is located. The project began as "Express 2000." At the same time, other countries such as Germany and France were also looking to update and modernize their import/export processing. Because the European Sponsor and others recognized the need to consider import/export processing on a global basis (or at least a European basis) rather than as separate country initiatives, they pushed to combine these European projects into one initiative called "Europe One." The scope of this project was very broad and included functions such as basic data capture, data control, and data distribution. To proceed with "Europe One," estimates from outside vendors were sought; the Import/Export Services development group of the company also prepared a bid. The project was awarded to Import/Export Services and the name changed to "the Shipments solution."

The Shipments solution is under development. The first increment (see discussion of increments in section III) has been funded locally, but the project team needs board approval and funding for the subsequent ten increments. At the time of this research, the project team is working on a high-level plan to present to the board to support the request for funding. If funding is denied, the project will be terminated.

C. The Project Team
The project team is organized in the following manner. The Project Manager, responsible for day-to-day management, is a senior systems advisor from an organizational unit that acts as a liaison between end users and IS. This group is located at worldwide headquarters. On a peer level with the Project Manager are several project coordinators; this group of individuals "ensures that the main interests being served by the project are properly represented at the working level" (project plan, 1997). The project coordinators include a European User Representative, a Technical Planning Advisor, and the Systems Development Manager who represent the business users, the planning function, and the technical organization respectively. Reporting directly to the Project Manager are the technical and business core team members, who do the actual work on the project. Each increment (see Section III) will have its own technical and business core teams.

The Project Manager, in turn, reports to a Project Board, consisting of three individuals: the European Sponsor of the project, the U.S. Sponsor, and the Technical Sponsor (who is the Managing Director of Import/Export Services). This board is responsible for approving the scope of the project, monitoring major milestones and deliverables, approving expenditures, resolving issues including shared business and technical-related concerns, making go/no go decisions, and ultimately ensuring the success of the project (project plan, 1997). The Project Board reports to a three-person Strategy Committee, which in turn reports to the Corporate Executive Strategy Committee, which includes the CIO.

This project team is organized to accommodate a special user liaison role. The European User Representative is one of the three project coordinators. He is responsible for facilitating communication between the regional IS unit (Import/Export Services) and the European users, who will receive the first implementation of the first increment. This representative visits the local sites and studies their operations, roles, and current systems. He feels that he needs to understand the local operations well enough to help with the local implementation of Shipments but at the same time understand the operations of all countries to keep a global perspective.

This on-site user liaison position has not been utilized in other projects at the company. The European User Representative is considered an extremely critical player in the project. Unlike the formal IS–end user liaison personnel, the European User Representative *directly* represents the end users. The developers, therefore, feel that they can get a better understanding of what the users need and want from the Shipments solution. The user representative commented that "any of the development team could just pop over to my desk and ask questions." The developers also feel that they can more directly communicate IS-related concerns to the end user community and can more satisfactorily resolve issues in a timely manner. A senior programmer analyst remarked that the European User Representative "is just like the man on the spot for the guys in Europe. You know, they're in constant contact to make sure that we're not forgetting anything, but so far we haven't."

D. Anticipated Project Outcomes

This company is in the process of identifying specific project outcomes. Although success criteria were not yet defined, most interviewees had their own vision of success. For example, a senior programmer analyst remarked:

> Real world success is a system where people are beating down your door saying, "Hey, we heard that this was available and we want that. Here's a bunch of money; give it to us." That's real world success. . . . There's another kind of success where everybody gets a medal and it's a declared success, . . . like you declare victory in Vietnam and get the hell out. And, I've seen a lot of declared successes that real people didn't want a thing to do with. And, to my view, real world success is that first kind. And so that's what I define success for this project as. And that's what I'm shooting for.

Formally, the project team has begun documenting and prioritizing success criteria in the project charter. The most important anticipated outcomes are related to reduce operating costs of both shipping processes and IT deployments as well as more efficient import/export shipping services. "Improved performance" is an identified anticipated outcome; however, no one can yet articulate exactly how improved performance will be measured. This company has also identified lower-priority project outcomes, including system reliability, user satisfaction, and on-time and within budget implementations.

III.   Deployment Strategies and Techniques

A. Development Methods and Processes

The general approach taken to the development of the Shipments solution is to build core pieces for all the common functions, with an open interface to allow regions to customize for language, regulations, and requirements such as electronic data interchange. The paradigm is standard technology, architecture, and tools combined with regional interface customization. Core functions are considered those needed to conduct the base business, whereas local pieces reflect the specific needs of the regions or countries.

Development teams will be geographically dispersed. The Import/Export systems team is responsible for developing the core pieces; the teams from multiple regions are responsible for customization (i.e., developing their own local pieces), as well as implementation and long-term support. Thus, all implementation and support tasks are the responsibility of the local IS units.

The approach to the development of the Shipments solution is referred to as an "incremental delivery approach." The entire project has been divided into a series of eleven increments, which may be developed in parallel or in sequence, depending upon technical issues and business priorities. The approach involves the following, as detailed in the 1997 project plan:

1. An overall plan.
2. An overall view of requirements.
3. An overall view of the data, technical, and user interface architectures.
4. Processes and procedures for the synchronization and management of the individual increments within an overall program.
5. Clear responsibility established for the management of the overall program.

Each increment will have its own project team, and each will be developed using a waterfall methodology, namely, business process definition, technical architecture definition, application definition, application engineering, and distributed deployment.

Within this company, there are standards organizations to ensure that new projects adhere to overall architectural requirements. For this project, the company is using a product called LBMS to identify tasks and estimate effort levels. LBMS provides process templates, methods, and techniques to assist in project management and systems development. This company is also using *Primavera* for project scheduling and tracking.

B. Rollout Strategies

Installing the Shipments solution means rolling out eleven implementations (i.e., deliverables from eleven increments) to 30 sites across 14 countries. It is anticipated that each site will be responsible for its local implementation. The Import/Export corporate team, who is responsible for developing the core pieces, will do no implementations; members will be available to help (possibly even on-site) but will not take responsibility. The Import/Export development team will build the parts and put them on the shelf; the parts will then be available for the local units to install when they decide to do so. The Managing Director of Import/Export Services describes the rollout and maintenance strategies as follows:

> I give you the transmission, but how you hook it up to the engine or bolt it onto the frame, I'm not going to get involved in necessarily. I will help and assist in, and consult if need be, but that responsibility and ownership needs to come from the region. And, as far as how they extend it . . . we're going to provide some guidelines, some controls to say, "Here's how you use the data," or, "This is how you have access." But we're not going to say, "Here's the core and here's the code that goes with it."

The first rollout for increment 1 will be in the United Kingdom, which is where the European sponsor of the Shipments solution is located. The specific rollout strategy has not yet been detailed, but it is anticipated that the needs of the local region will dictate when their first implementations occur.

C. Maintenance and Support Strategies

At present, each site is expected to take on responsibility for maintenance and support of the local part of the system and the local hardware and telecommunications infrastructure. The Import/Export development group will support the core pieces, providing ongoing support for that part of the Shipments solution. The Systems Development Manager anticipates that, due to limited resources of the Import/Export Services application development group, two versions of the core increments will be maintained at any time.

IV.   Challenges and Resolutions

A. Selling the Solution

In the early days of this project, when it was a European initiative, the European Sponsor spent considerable time trying to bring together the different European countries to work together. Initially, she found them reluctant to cooperate on a European project; each country wanted its own solution. There were instances of individuals not attending meetings because a particular country representative was there! Several factors helped bring the individual parties together: the European Sponsor's relentless efforts, the explicit support of upper management of the European division, and the ongoing European Union initiatives. At the time of the case, the European region had bought into the project and agreed to fund increment number 1.

As the project progressed, the team and management actively sought buy-in from other locations. At least one user meeting was held to solicit that buy in. The outcome was the commitment from two regions that had actively resisted the Shipments effort. According to the Systems Development Manager:

> The purpose of this [user] meeting was gaining consensus. It's an education process. There was lots of discussion on what was happening, what will be gained, and so on. There was upper management support, saying essentially that this is it, there is no choice. If you want a global [Shipments] solution, this is it. We had a VP there, who was very supportive. He said the Board package would include all the regional needs, that there would be funds for the regions [who will] need to increase staffing, development, equipment. That funding would be included in the Board package. It would be presented as a global project.

With the support of the various regions, the project team now must develop a high-level plan, including a budget, and submit it to the board to secure funding for the entire project. Along with the plan, the project team must provide evidence of the feasibility and soundness of the project and must be able to articulate the benefits or cost reductions that the Shipments solution will enable. Since the first increment is being developed outside of this board package, the project team will use the knowledge gained from that "mini" project to build its business case for the rest of the Shipments solution.

B. Building Global Ownership for the Shipments Solution

One of the major challenges facing this company is how to build global ownership for the Shipments solution. Historically, the company has deployed systems for individual countries or regions, even when those systems have provided largely the same functionality. With the deployment of the Shipments solution, this practice of building and implementing individual systems for individual countries is changing. For the first time, the company is identifying the core business processes across regions and providing a common solution that the regions can then adapt to local needs.

With respect to the current status of the Shipments solution, the Managing Director of Import/Export Services noted that the global ownership does not yet exist: "I think the ownership is still in Europe. I think the sponsorship is still in Europe. I think the Project Manager's organization is more in a support role." He also stressed how important global ownership is to the Shipments solution:

> I think that one of the biggest things that will probably determine the success is how can you get some ownership on a global basis. And, get people out of the mode of saying, "Hey, I'm going to kind of control it and kind of stamp my name on it and have it look like I want to look."

Exactly how global ownership is going to occur is not clear at this point. A couple of the individuals interviewed argued that global ownership results from one-on-one negotiating between IS and functional area managers from the different regions but, more importantly, sponsorship from senior business managers who mandate common business processes and standard ways of operating.

C. Controlling and Coordinating the Process
There are numerous formal control and coordination mechanisms in place for this project. They include quarterly meetings of the Project Board to review milestones and so on, weekly progress meetings held by the increment project lead, and biweekly meetings between IS and the users held by the Project Manager. There are quality standards—for the platform and for the process—that articulate the technological requirements. Tools and methodologies also help to control and coordinate the process. For example, on a weekly basis, team members receive messages generated by *Primavera,* a project management software tool, that details out their tasks for the week.

Other means of controlling and coordinating the process include kick-off meetings, which serve to lay out a reasonable mission and individual responsibilities. During the kick-off meetings, the following are also articulated: the nature of individual contributions, the challenge to everyone to perform well, the challenge to individuals to continually learn, and the expectations that everyone will be able to accomplish the goals. This company, in turn, formally recognizes and rewards high-performing teams and individuals.

Some of these control and coordination mechanisms are aimed only at the Import/Export staff working on the core pieces. For example, project progress reports, reviews, sign-offs, and so on related to the *core pieces* are destined for or attended by just Import/Export staff located in the United States. To keep the European counterparts in the loop, conference calls are held regularly. The increment project lead holds at least weekly conversations with her European counterparts. All project documentation is also distributed to all locations. Additionally, a proof of concept test was conducted in the United Kingdom, using the hardware and software architecture of these sites to ensure that the Shipments solution technology would work.

This project team tried videoconferencing as a control and coordination technique, but it found the technology ineffective: "We've tried it a couple of times, but our lines to Europe are so bad and the delay is so awful, it just makes it worse because people get frustrated" (senior technical advisor). The team prefers to travel, having face-to-face meetings, to coordinate work and resolve issues.

Formal organizational positions also facilitate the control and coordination of the Shipments solution project. The overall Project Manager, for example, is part of a formal organizational unit that provides liaison support between IS and the users. In addition, the European User Representative plays a control and coordination role by facilitating the discussion between the Import/Export group and the European user organizations, in particular, the U.K. folks. The European User Representative is effective because of his location (in the United States, with the Import/Export developers), because of his past relationship with the European Sponsor (they worked together in Canada) and because of his knowledge of the business area.

Besides the formal control and coordination mechanisms, in this company individuals also rely on informal approaches. Most individuals interviewed, in fact, felt that they used many more informal mechanisms than formal ones. They estimated that 90 to 95 percent of the mix was informal. In contrast, the Managing Director of Import/Export Services indicated that he used about half formal and half informal control and coordination strategies.

Some of the informal means of control and coordination included making people feel a part of the team, social events, more informal than formal reviews, and traveling. While several individuals noted the importance of informal control and coordination, they also noted that a prime barrier to this approach is that individuals are not co-located. This problem is heightened by the fact that individuals are quite distant—not just one or two time zones away. To at least partially address this problem, all U.S. developers were co-located on one floor of one building; the Import/Export developers had previously been spread over several locations. The Systems Development Manager commented on how helpful co-location is:

> I can see the people interacting. The people get together immediately, instead of saying "I'll meet you at 3:00.". . . This is an indicator of improved productivity.

Several people mentioned how important past personal relationships were to getting the work done. If the history isn't there, they noted, they would have to spend more time cultivating that relationship and/or relying on formal mechanisms of control and coordination. The Systems Development Manager noted: "I think personal relationships are the grease and the lubricant that make it all work smoothly. . . . And, the more tightly machined something is, the less lubrication is necessary. So, it's kind of offset [a trade-off]." Similarly, explaining his relationship to the European User Representative, a senior programmer analyst commented:

> [He] and I are old pals from [a previous project]. And, he's got the juice to say to local management and technicians that: "Hey, it ought to be this way, [for me to] sign off. This thing you're coming up with isn't going to fly." . . . And, I'm kind of handicapped in that I can't persuade anybody of anything. I couldn't persuade somebody to leave a burning house, you know, I just can't do it. But I can persuade [the European User Representative] because, you know, he's been through it with me. . . . So that's been real handy from my point of view to have that avenue for getting something done.

In general, with respect to control and coordination, many of the issues are the same, regardless of whether the projects are global. That is, control and coordination are difficult because of the number of people involved; the complexities of the project; the spread of knowledge among project participants; and the difficulties associated with determining requirements, managing change, and forging consensus. All of these difficulties are still there and are, in fact, heightened by the global nature of the project (the time difference, the differences in culture, and the differences in infrastructures).

D. Working in a Global Environment

Besides the issues mentioned in the preceding section, other difficulties were discussed. First, the difference in time zones creates problems of logistics: There are just not many hours in the day when individuals can communicate in "real time."

Second, several individuals commented on the differences in meanings of analysis and design. The U.S. and U.K. counterparts hold conflicting views on what constitutes a complete analysis and a complete design. For example, the U.S. developers conducted a more detailed analysis while their U.K. counterparts conducted a high-level conceptual analysis. Therefore, when reviewing the U.K. documents, the U.S. developers felt the analysis was incomplete and spent a considerable amount of extra time in the analysis phase. On the other hand, the U.K. developers produced an extremely detailed design that included code-level documents with every field and level name identified. The U.K. developers felt that the U.S. design documents were too vague and complained that they could not code from them. This difference in viewpoints prompted considerable discussion about the meaning of analysis and design. The resolution of this issue was to separate the tasks; the U.S. group took on the task of developing the core modules, and the U.K. group assumed responsibility for their local adaptations.

Third, there are differences in tool sets. One location was accustomed to using *Power Builder* for client side interfaces, while another location preferred *UNIFACE*. In this particular instance, the decision to use *Power Builder* was, in essence, a mandate from upper management. One explanation given for the differences in both analysis/design methods and tool sets involved the type or size of system typically deployed by the U.S. staff as opposed to those deployed by the U.K group. Since U.S. developers had done most application development at this company, they were more accustomed to large and complex systems. In contrast, the U.K. (and other non-U.S.) regions had mostly developed simpler and smaller systems. Thus, the methods and tools used by the U.S. staff tended to be appropriate for big systems; this was not generally true of the methods and tools used by other development groups.

A fourth issue is finding skilled personnel for all locations. The IS organization (in particular, the Import/Export Services group) has tried to empower local units to do some of their own work. But because the local units often have difficulties finding people, they often subcontract the work back to the company's corporate IS employees. The Managing Director of Import/Export indicated that he had a number of people who are directly funded or working for the non-U.S. regions on local applications.

Finally, the company is struggling with approaches to sharing responsibilities. They are ambivalent about who is ultimately responsible for the project, with several of those interviewed suggesting different people were responsible for different pieces. Moreover, they are concerned about how to share responsibility for implementation and for long-term support. At this point, they are uncertain about what is the best approach to sharing responsibility and what, in fact, is workable. The Managing Director summarized his feelings as follows:

> It's not been very easy to do [sharing responsibility]. I would say that at least from a technical standpoint, I own responsibility of the development, implementation. Some of the other parts—as far as making sure that the funding is there, making sure that the business has processes in place—that's where we typically run into problems. . . . It's really a shared responsibility between IT and the business to make sure that happens.

E. Managing Change

With the implementation of the Shipments solutions, the local sites will receive both new technology and new business processes. The project manager explains that reengineering and the technology implementation go hand in hand. He comments that one part of the project is "reengineering or looking at the total flow and process, and change how we do the business. Then, the other half is a systems side to say: 'Okay, if we change our flow of business this way, then the system comes in and supports it.'" It is critical to understand the relationship of reengineering business processes and technology implementations. The project manager explains:

> You can't just come in and say, "Here's a new system." It won't work. You can't just come in and say, "We're going to change this process." It won't work. Yes, it may make things better, but it's not the total piece. So, it's a combination.

The Managing Director notes that the implementation of the Shipments solution affects virtually every location, and it represents a large change as more and more of the import/export processing is automated and the work environment becomes paperless. The project team members are expecting to meet some resistance as the Shipments solution is rolled out. As the senior technical advisor notes

> Each country has defined their own procedures, standard operating procedures, and it's different by country. They take things that we at corporate give them as tools and then implement them their own way. And that's a major stumbling block when we walk in and say, "Okay, you have to change all your procedures around."

To address this resistance, a team will go to the local site before the technical implementation to make the changes to the operating procedures. The goal is to institute global standard operating procedures.

F. Maintaining the Global Solution

Managers anticipate that the local units will assume responsibility for maintaining and supporting the local application, hardware, and infrastructure while the global team will be accountable for the core and common pieces. This type of split responsibility is new, and, at this point, it is not clear how easy it will be for the various units to pinpoint the source of the problems (i.e., whether it is a local problem or a core problem). The Managing Director of Import/Export Systems indicated that this area is one of his biggest concerns about the deployment of the Shipments solution.

With respect to maintaining the core and common pieces, the expectation is that a limited and small (e.g., two) number of versions will be supported at any one time. The implication is that when new versions of common and core components are developed, the local sites must implement them, regardless of whether the updated versions address their specific needs. The director recognizes that persuading regions to upgrade may be difficult, especially if a region has no need for the enhanced or additional functionality that is embedded in the upgrade. He believes that the rollout and maintenance strategies must be articulated, communicated, and sold to the regions:

> I think we have to sell the whole deployment strategy up front. We have to convince people that if they are going to implement this system at all, then they have to keep up with the upgrades. . . . We have to convince them of our limited resources to do everything, and of their need to commit to being a part of the global solution.

G. Demonstrating the Efficacy of the Deployment Process

The project team's deployment approach—the incremental development process, with the global team developing core and common components and the local team adding local functionality and installing the solution—is new. While the team is confident that this approach will be effective, it also wants to demonstrate the viability of the approach. The hope is that this approach will decrease the costs of deploying and maintaining technology-based solutions. The Systems Development manager explains that a successful deployment process is one that delivers a useful product and that is repeatable across all increments.

The PRODUCTION Solution

I.   Background

The Production solution was implemented by a firm that is a leader in health care supply distribution, manufacturing, and management services. The headquarters of the company is in the United States, but it has over 25 manufacturing plants around the world and over 20,000 employees worldwide. Net revenues for 1996 were over $4 billion. This company manufactures and distributes thousands of medical, surgical, and laboratory products in sufficient diversity to be able to fill most of a typical hospital's supply needs. The company manufactures surgical gloves, drapes, gowns, and other single-use apparel products; surgical instruments; custom sterile product kits; respiratory-therapy products; and a range of other medical products (catheters, collection tubing and canisters, etc.). The company distributes its self-manufactured products as well as products from other suppliers, and it ships approximately 900,000 boxes of supplies to more than 6,000 locations per day. The company offers just-in-time delivery systems for hospitals that want to lower their inventory storage and management costs. The fastest-growing segment of the company is cost management services. Company consultants work with hospital staff to standardize and reduce supply use (average annual cost savings of 20 percent) and to improve clinical and business operations.

The corporate officers at the company include a Chairman and CEO, a COO, a CFO, a CIO, and four other corporate vice presidents (human resources, quality, strategy, and regional operations). The corporate information systems group reports to the CIO and includes over 150 people. In addition, there are IS functions within every business area, which tend to be smaller, less formal organizations. The vice president in charge of each of these business area functions reports to the CIO. Both the corporate and business unit IS groups are, in the words of one user, "expected to be a full business partner," with a rich understanding of the business and much on-site interaction with users in the business units.

II.   Solution and Project Description

A. The Project: Goals, Objectives, and Drivers

The Production solution, based on the integrated package PRMS, drives manufacturing processes and controls at the company. Specific functions of PRMS include accounts payable, general ledger, shop floor control, purchasing, materials management, capacity planning, and labor planning and reporting. At the company, data from the distribution network for the whole company are input into the system. Based on information from the distribution sites and sales, the system produces a master production schedule and work orders. The system tracks and accounts for work in progress through the production process until finished goods are shipped to a distribution center.

There were four major drivers for the Production solution. The primary driver was high inventory cost. Before the Production solution was implemented, business units maintained a "huge pipeline" of inventory: on average, Division 1 had between 200 to 280 days and Division 2 had between 130 to 140 days of shipping inventory. At the same time, the company experienced real cost pressures from major competitors (e.g., one such competitor took 30 percent of the business away at one point through lower-cost products).

A second driver was poor information flow. In the early 1990s, an outside consulting firm tried to document the current information flow for the manufacturing process, and "it looked like a bowl of spaghetti." The consulting firm thought that the reason the company was not doing adequate production and materials planning and not meeting production schedules was an information flow so complicated that it didn't work. The company had to go to many different people at many locations in order to get information needed to manage manufacturing.

Poor sharing of data was another driver for the solution. Each department and functional area throughout the business units had its own PC-based systems, each with its own data, in addition to a corporate, mainframe supply manufacturing system. These systems produced what each department wanted, but in the words of the project manager, "when you look at the quality of data in it, they weren't getting the right solutions that they were looking for." There was much rekeying of data or no common data or data standards, and support of the various systems was costly and difficult. One planning manager says that while "each department really optimized their areas, where it fell apart was at month-end close, when they tried to reconcile inventory balances in the warehouse to what was in the systems, and it often took ten days to close."

There were also conflicts between departments when data were shared; each department thought part of the problem was that other departments either did not give them what they needed or did not use the data they gave them correctly: "And they would scream at other departments, 'You're not keeping my data.' And that just seemed to be rampant throughout the company" (project manager).

There were no inventory data shared electronically from nondomestic sites, which replenished inventory by placing monthly orders. Because the manufacturing of some items, in particular gloves, is distributed throughout the world, there are often considerable manufacturing lead times, which can result in low inventory levels or even outages if inventories are kept low. Again, this led to the maintenance of uneconomically high inventory levels.

Finally, the perception that poor information prevented growth was another driver. The initial PRMS implementation was championed by the controller of a business area, who wanted to grow that area but felt he couldn't because of inventory and production problems caused by the poor information flows and lack of accurate shared data.

B. Project History

In 1986, a project manager was brought in by the controller to find an integrated manufacturing package to run this business. A cross-functional team was created to evaluate the packages on the market at that time, and PRMS was selected. All departments of this business area, with between 40 and 50 users, were automated by the end of 1987. "It was very successful. We immediately turned around the issues that they had in their production department. We immediately turned around the problems they had in their technical service department, got links for their sales department and the controller was promoted . . . to the . . . division" (project manager).

The promoted controller brought the project manager to corporate to replicate the PRMS implementation throughout the business units, which had similar problems on a larger scale. The project in the Division 1 business (in the United States only) started in May 1989, and the system was running by November 1989. From 1990 to 1993, the Production solution was implemented in Division 3 manufacturing plants in the United States and Puerto Rico. Concurrent with Division 3 deployment (1991 to 1994), the solution was implemented in the largest manufacturing operation in the company, Division 2. (This one part of the business is larger than other textile companies such as Levi-Strauss.) One aspect of this implementation that made it technically more difficult is that each plant does not operate independently, but clusters of plants share manufacturing processes. Division 2 sites are located throughout the United States and Mexico. The last major implementation of the Production solution, begun in 1993, is in the glove business part of Division 2, with plants in Malaysia, Singapore, Costa Rica, Mexicali, and the United States The Production solution is currently in maintenance phase for most company locations.

There are two projects ongoing to add functionality to the Production solution. First the corporate systems group is working to make the information on company inventory and distribution/sales visible to its suppliers so that instead of the company placing purchase orders with suppliers, the major suppliers will look at inventory levels and outflow and projections and ship products appropriately. This linkage to suppliers will use a third-party EDI connection. The second project concerns the development of the master production schedule, which currently is being based on inventory levels and set replenish levels. This project, which should take about nine months, will allow the company to automatically create what the systems manager for one division calls a "true master production schedule" with minimal planning specialist input to the process.

C. Project Teams
The project teams for each deployment of PRMS at the company were cross-functional. For example, the team to deploy PRMS in the Division 2 business was headed by a project manager who had project responsibility and organized the team. He recruited a businessperson from Division 2 to be the champion and an accounting manager from one manufacturing plant (both of whom spent 80 to 90 percent of their time on the project). In addition, the team included a buyer, the purchasing manager, materials manager, the quality director, a representative from each of the Mexican plants, a person from the general office at corporate, a plant manager, the director of Division 2 business, one systems manager, a business systems consultant, and three programmers. These project team members from the business areas had a part-time involvement. There were also two other IS people who worked one site for about six months at a time during implementation. During implementation, a team was formed with local users and managers combined with the IS people from corporate.

The team met at least monthly to review status and discuss issues to be resolved. These issues usually meant team members had to go back and gather information from their constituency or they had to discuss and resolve cross-area problems in information flows. Often these meetings were in conjunction with the weekly or monthly staff meetings of the director of manufacturing. Project team member bonuses were tied to successful system implementation.

D. Project Outcomes
There is consensus that the Production solution is a great improvement over the previous situation of multiple independent systems, but it is not considered by all to be an unequivocal success. The

Production solution is considered a success for several reasons. First, the company has realized the expected cost savings from operations and inventory efficiencies (number of days in inventory for Division 2 is now 54 this year, and next year the goal is 34) and since inventory in transit between plants is also tracked, there are reduced material variances. Second, all the manufacturing data are in one place. Third, because every manufacturing plant is on a consistent software and hardware platform, there is maximum flexibility in human resources: "We have taken our business from a discrete work center environment to a cellular environment" (project manager). Fourth, cost information from the Production solution is used to sell products. For example, data are analyzed across customers to identify lowest-cost surgical kits for the 300 most common surgical procedures. These data are then used when marketing kits to hospitals.

The system is not considered a total success for several reasons. One systems manager from corporate IS says that people who did not experience the old situation and its problems do not see that the Production solution is a vast improvement but in fact think of it as "business as usual." The project manager thinks many people have unrealistic "Star Trek–type" expectations for what a system can reasonably do. One business analyst who was on the project and implementation teams believes that more sophisticated, 'information-hungry" users lead to dissatisfaction with any system. The director of manufacturing for one division reported that many people think that because there have been many add-on applications and the interfaces with other applications are not totally smooth, the system is "piecemeal" and not fully integrated. The immediate impact on some users, especially first-line supervisors in the manufacturing plants whose jobs were expanded, and the system implementation led to significant turnover. While a few employees were excited about the possibilities, about 25 percent tolerated the change, and about 50 to 60 percent left the company or changed jobs.

The installation of the Production solution in Division 1 was on time and within the $1 billion budgeted for the project. At Division 3, half the plants were installed on schedule, but the others were late. The project manager attributes the lateness to the fact that solution implementation was not a priority for the then vice president of manufacturing of Division 3, and he delayed it 18 months. He was actually trying to run both legacy systems and put in *PRMS*, and was paying for both. He was fired, and the replacement made the switch to the Production solution a high priority.

The Division 2 installation was six months late and $200,000 over the $3 million budget. The major problem with this installation stemmed from the inability to convert inventory data from the old system to new system as initially planned. This technical problem was leading to variances of $13 million, so two days into cutover, the conversion had to be stopped, and it took 60 days to resolve the problem.

III.   Deployment Strategies and Techniques
A. Development Methods and Processes
This firm implemented *PRMS*, an integrated package for manufacturing and process control. *PRMS* was initially a product of Pansofic (Pansofic Resource Management System), written for IBM System 38s. About four years ago, Pansofic was purchased by Computer Associates. *PRMS* is used in all divisions of this company and currently runs on AS/400s. The adaptation of *PRMS* to run on AS/400s was done by IBM.

The project to deploy *PRMS* in the company was done incrementally by business area. There was no initial master plan to implement an integrated package throughout the company. Instead, the package was successfully deployed in one relatively small business area ($40 to 50 million in sales), and when the champion (the controller) was promoted to a corporate level, the companywide rollout began.

B. Rollout Strategies

At each location there was a local implementation team of about 35 people, with representatives from every department. Responsibility for each piece of information was assigned to a director of a business area, and when information was shared across areas, the directors resolved differences and assigned responsibility between them. During rollout, training was staged by first training a few key users (usually departmental supervisors), who then trained the others. The reason for this was lack of adequate· time for training. But several interviewees reported that the hurried training caused problems, including some of the delays and turnover.

C. Maintenance and Support Strategies

Maintenance and support are handled by a layered local and corporate combined support system. Day-to-day problems are fielded first by the technical IS staff located at each site. If that staff cannot fix the problem, then the systems professionals for the plant clusters are responsible. Problems that cannot be solved at these local levels are sent to the divisional IS staff. Any problems still not resolved, or solutions that should be shared globally, are sent to corporate IS.

Upgrades to the *PRMS* by the vendor are planned via a formal project. The project team includes corporate and divisional IS staff as well as users. The team evaluates whether the upgrade should be made, as well as how the upgrade will impact the add-on systems that the company has developed as part of the solution. For example, current maintenance activity centers on the upgrade to version 8.4, which will take care of the year 2000 problem. This upgrade project is scheduled to last six months, because it is a major upgrade and the systems staff has to figure out the impact on the ten to twelve "home-grown" (i.e., company-developed) applications that add functionality to the basic product. These applications change over time, since in some cases they add functionality before a new version of the product does. For example, the company had an application that automatically created purchase orders to suppliers when appropriate that will be superseded by the new version of *PRMS* that has this feature built in.

IV.   Challenges and Resolutions

A. Building Global Ownership

For each deployment of the Production solution, there was a conscious attempt to build ownership of the system and the need for it in the business units. The process began with a big kickoff meeting of everyone to explain the overview of what the system will look like. The systems users used the spaghetti diagram of their current information flow that had been prepared by the consultants and showed the business managers the new one with *PRMS*. According to one corporate planning manager, users really tried to sell the idea of *one* data base for everyone, as well as prepare people for the new manufacturing processes. The manufacturing director for one division said that the key strategy was to communicate the mutual benefit for all units and that the larger challenge (in comparison to building the system) was to properly understand what each organization needs from one another. This was critical to selling system users on the need to cooperate and make it clear that they are not being asked to "be the same for the sake of being the same."

Within the project team, there were also efforts to build ownership and accountability. For example, during the project, every issue raised in a project meeting was assigned a champion with responsibility for the issue and a deadline for resolution. These issues were quite specific (e.g., resolving what the truck/trailer numbers are going to be for transit of work in progress between sites that are in different countries). If a deadline was missed twice, the person responsible was taken off the team and replaced.

Local implementation teams also tried to give the system visibility by naming it (e.g., Division 2 was mainly in Mexico, so they called it "Cima," which means "the top") and using that name in monthly status reports and in newsletters. Interestingly, the project manager reported that the teams had an easier time building ownership of the system with the Mexican plant managers because they saw it as a career opportunity rather than just a technical installation project.

B. Controlling and Coordinating the Process

Both formal and information techniques of control and coordination were employed. An example of a formal method was the fact that managers' bonuses were tied to system success; the project manager commented, "I got in their pocketbooks, and I mean a substantial piece of their pocketbooks, so I had their attention going in." At all levels people understood that they had to adjust to the new system or be gone.

There was substantial use of informal techniques. Sometimes this was because no formal mechanisms were available. For example, at the lower levels of the organization, managers could not offer financial compensation, so they used an array of techniques. The project manager noted that "a lot of times, just taking the time to talk through it with them, they'd go off and be very motivated to get that problem resolved." Other approaches were communication to the team members that this was a career opportunity to be able to do something new, gifts to compensate for extra work and effort (rented golf clubs, pens, t-shirts, dinners), humor (the project manager told jokes, danced on the table if a team member caught him in any kind of error). All individuals interviewed who participated in the on-site implementation said they tried to establish rapport on a personal level to build trust. They felt it required two or three weeks to build trusting relationships. Because they were on-site for long periods of time during deployment, their day-to-day contact really helped build strong and effective relationships.

C. Managing Change

Prior to deployment of the Production solution, within each functional area and across areas there were different, independent systems and data. The project manager remarked that it was very hard to eliminate these systems:

> The department heads were convinced that these PC systems were their salvation. They developed them specifically for the number of people they had . . . but they never got a good source of information.

The resolution was to mandate change, and so the project manager became a "dictator":

> [I] laid out what that strategy was and where the sources of all these databases would be, and told them that they [the users] had to such and such a date to get off the system they're on and move on to the next one. If you can't get off, you will be gone and your replacement will find a way to adapt.

In addition, the director of manufacturing mandated use by refusing to take reports with data from old systems and required data from *PRMS*.

The Production solution required many large changes in the way business was done. A plant manager in a cross-border manufacturing cluster described how many people who were quite effective in the old manual system in filling out forms for their piece of the operation were unable to enter and reconcile data on the entire transaction. With the Production solution, his line managers had to open and close the work order as well as reconcile work orders against materials usage variances and inventory. The plant managers did not anticipate this job expansion. A system manager for that division reports that this was made worse by too little training and preparation for the change from a "four-walled system" to a system of managing discrete orders across plant locations. This was, according to the project manager, the first time anyone had made employees at many levels understand a companywide strategy. The use of the solution was mandated, so these problems did not lead to nonuse, but the resolution for many first-line managers was that they left or changed jobs.

Resistance in some cases was not to the information system but to the processes it embodied. A business analyst on the project reported that in some Mexican plants, processing was fairly loose and so structuring work along basic manufacturing best practices was difficult. There was also resistance to any information that would direct the plant manager to shut down a line for awhile because they did not want to send people home (i.e., they did not want their employees to lose wages). Despite this, the Mexican plants did not have as high a mortality rate as U.S. plants from the implementation, and in fact, these plant managers viewed the changes in processing embodied in the move to the Production solution as an opportunity to advance their careers.

D. Dealing with Turnover

The team experienced a lot of turnover, with almost every position turning over two or three times. (This was a time of great turnover in the Division 2 business.) This presented a problem, because as the group membership changed (especially when the change was in a business user representative), requirements changed. The project manager was really the only constant. Because of this turnover in the project team, he says, "this was the worst, hardest project I've been involved in! This was without a doubt, harder than all the other projects I've ever done added together."

E. Engendering Commitment of Managers at Local Level

There was, in some cases, a lack of commitment to the project by local upper-level plant managers. This lack of commitment was attributed by the business analyst to those managers' distance from the nitty-gritty day-to-day problems; they didn't see the benefit to themselves and so the project was a low priority. In those locations, however, middle managers were committed because they did see the benefits. In some plants, the impact of this commitment disjoint was that they got behind schedule, missing deadlines. These plants had to scramble to get the project done. The ultimate successful implementation in those plants was at least in part due to the willingness of middle managers to do double work to get it done.

F. Addressing Cultural Differences

Members of the implementation teams were not bilingual, nor had they had prior experience in other countries/cultures, and so those members who were interviewed all reported making special efforts to communicate effectively. The project manager spoke in particular about the need to be sensitive to differences in culture when conducting business meetings. For example, he realized that with Mexican managers, he needed to spend about ten minutes at the beginning of a meeting talking about family and sharing pictures before moving on to the business discussion. A systems manager's approach was to identify a key individual to work with who believed in the system and could learn it and to focus on building a close relationship with that individual. Once that person was an ally, he or she could help "translate" with the other employees. A business analyst also felt that developing a small cohort group while co-located on-site gave her that mechanism for communication throughout and after the implementation.

G. Maintaining the System

There is overt concern about maintaining the common processes and system globally. One set of concerns relates to the *PRMS* package itself, the other to its relationship to other systems at the company. There is an expressed "fear that over time we will be back to where we started, with islands of automation" and that it is a "challenge to be sure there is just one *[PRMS]* package running in all locations" (a systems manager). This systems manager estimates that about 95 to 97 percent of the *PRMS* package is the same across all installations, ignoring differences in format or language of reports and input screens. Division 1 in particular has many "bolt-on" adaptations for local needs throughout the sites. Some of these were in how the data were collected (bar code readers, radio frequency devices) or in how local physical arrangements required adaptations to the standard package. Other differences come from plants that hired consultants to write applications for what they view as unique needs. Both a systems manager and planning manager remarked that since they allowed some local variation in the system initially, this has encouraged local users to develop their own add-ons. These adaptations were completely justifiable, but they have caused problems, in particular during package upgrades. The project manager emphasized a broader need to utilize packages and minimize local customization:

> In order to be competitive, I feel that you've got to determine that your company is not in the software business. And you've got to attach yourself to somebody who is. Because if you don't, I'm going to tell you, your competition *is*.

The company is employing two approaches to maintaining the Production solution as a common global system. First, it has identified the plant managers as "champions of consistency" who are responsible for reinforcing the need to keep the systems and processes common across all plants. Second, the corporate systems manager tries to support the local applications (e.g., during upgrades to the package) and to evaluate local innovations for possible implementation in all locations. He commented, "If it is a good idea, it should be shared and put as an option in all locations, especially since there is a cost to the company to create and maintain such local features."

There is also concern about the relationship of *PRMS* to the company's *SAP R/3* rollout. The decision was made to stay with the Production solution and to interface *PRMS* to *R/3*. In fact, the ability to create that interface was critical to the selection of *R/3*. The corporate systems manager interviewed believes that interfacing the two products is good because it means that there will be an even tighter link in the whole pipeline and that an indirect effect is that customer service in the regions should have better information about manufacturing. He says the reason the company didn't make the switch now to using *R/3*'s manufacturing modules instead of *PRMS* is cost, which is estimated to be about $10 million to convert plus the additional costs of changing the users' world again. But he wondered whether or not that decision will hold five years from now and asked, "Does it *[PRMS]* outlive its usefulness in five to ten years?"

The ENTERPRISE Solution

I.   Background

The company implementing the Enterprise solution is a chemical manufacturing firm with $2.5 billion in yearly sales. The company has two main business groups. The bulk of the business is in producing standard products. In this part of the business, the focus is on products with established operational excellence, and the company competes on price and on its ability to react to customers' increasing expectations of better service. The second part of the business is oriented toward product innovation and draws on the company's knowledge base in its particular chemical area. In this part of the business, it tends to partner with other companies to develop products for customers that employ this chemical product.

For many years, this company dominated its niche in the chemical industry. As the number of competitors increased, especially in the more profitable parts of the market, the company did not change because it was still growing and profitable. However, in the early 1990s, the company faced a significant crisis in the form of a product liability claim although the claim was unsubstantiated by scientific evidence. Some view this crisis as having a positive effect, creating a climate ripe for change. The crisis created a sense of urgency, and employees realized that the company could lose its market dominance or even fail completely. The situation caused employees to rally in support of the management team by openly expressing their support in a newspaper ad and by not leaving the company.

II.   Solution and Project Description

A. The Project: Goals, Objectives, and Drivers

The Enterprise solution is a global, full functionality implementation of *SAP R/3* and is described as "the most far-reaching strategic change initiative that the company has ever undertaken. It aims to ensure our continued ability to grow and prosper worldwide." This project has the number 1 priority position in the company because it is viewed as creating a platform that will enable significant reengineering gains. This created a business pull for the *SAP* implementation and has driven a very aggressive implementation schedule (initially 2000; now set for 1998). Two reasons for implementing *SAP* worldwide by the end of 1998 are that the company is not fixing year 2000 problems in the legacy systems and the difficulty in sustaining this kind of effort and change for very long time periods.

This cost-reduction/avoidance driver for the Enterprise solution fits in with the overall business strategy for reducing costs in the standard product end of the business. The support for all business processes globally with one system is also viewed as helping the company make customer service more even across locations.

Another key driver is the need for the company to make the transition to operating on a global supply chain basis, away from the historical functional area orientation (described as "a major cultural twist for us"). The project manager believes this will yield economies as well as serve customers better. The role of IT is to put the common platform in place, and then business leadership must "seize the opportunities and make them happen."

Change in Business Processes. The decision was made to "stair step" major business process changes along with the implementation of *SAP R/3*. That is, the company is using the implementation of *R/3* as a means of forcing changes in business processes. The project manager described the project process:

"We're going to act, we're going to learn, and we're going to design" as opposed to the traditional engineering approach of learning, designing, acting. This required a "cultural shift," since as engineers the managers would have preferred to study first, then make a choice, and then implement.

B. The Project Team

The project team got together as a group in July through September 1995 and struggled. A new project manager was appointed in January 1996, and the project team was restructured in June 1996. The organization is skill based with global process coordinators who have responsibility for a chunk of functionality, usually tied to one of the four business processes (customer focus, product delivery, finance, HR). The global process coordinators work with the business process managers and area business sponsors to prioritize functional requirements and obtain resources to meet those needs.

The core group is located centrally. Some people are distributed and come to the central global location for periods (a month to six weeks at a time). Some members of the global team are also members of the area teams (described later).

The global team is responsible for defining global workflows and developing the functionality and the configuration. The team also participates in implementation, doing about 20 percent of the work. The global team provides support for the area teams, and if the area team lacks skill or knowledge, the global team supplies it. Also, a special training facility is designed to train the area teams and local power users to work the functionality and configuration.

The global project team includes a mix of business process and IT people and, according to the project manager, this team has "a pretty good balance of people who really recognize what these opportunities are" (i.e., the vision of transforming the company). One team member noted that sometimes an individual is viewed as a businessperson, when he or she actually started on the IT side, and many of the businesspeople have quite technical backgrounds and lots of project experience. One process coordinator noted that while the mix of business and technical backgrounds is good, sometimes the business members resist getting into *SAP* in the depth that is needed. The global process coordinator role is mainly administrative: keeping the project on track, constructing the project plan, maintaining the functionality list, and assigning deadlines.

The head of IT in Europe is responsible for implementing the Enterprise solution in Europe and with his European process directors forms a steering committee for process management. The committee's role in negotiating with local sites is discussed later in this document.

The responsibility for the hardware infrastructure, data loading, programming reports, and user exits, as well as other technical support, is provided by a separate IT group that reports to the head of IT. There are dotted line relationships with people on the global project team.

The area implementation teams for the three areas (America, Asia, Europe) are made up of power users—resident experts in the areas who are businesspeople with heavy IT knowledge and who are assigned to the Enterprise solution full-time for between two and four months. One key role for the power users is that they prepare all the data to be loaded into *SAP*. This task involves much data cleaning. Power users, some of whom are IT professionals, are identified by the local sites. No formal selection process is used, and the head of IT says that these people tend to be "recognized as experienced and competent people on their part of the process" and, to some extent, "they've selected themselves."

Area teams have responsibility for implementation, since the global team is really responsible only for developing functionality and configuration. Area teams are responsible for preparing sites for change, so it is critical that they understand where the changes are going to be made and how radical the change in work flows will be. They are also responsible for holding change management meetings two to three months before implementation. A formal role in the site implementation is the Optimization Leader of the area team, who monitors the impact of the site implementation in terms of productivity, overtime, how *SAP* is used, and additional training needs. He forwards his findings and an action plan to the area implementation leader.

C. Project History

Prior to the Enterprise project, the company partially developed and implemented a global order entry system. In most locations, this order entry system never went beyond a plan, but in the European area, a small part of it was implemented. There were many conflicts over what was going to be done and how, and since everything was possible in an in-house developed system, it was easy for everyone to argue for his or her way. The scope expanded quickly until "we really had a system that was meant to do anything and everything for everyone" (team member). Many of the Enterprise solution team members (estimated at 40 percent) also worked on this order entry system.

One member of the team thinks this previous experience was one reason the company decided not to try to build global solutions in-house but to purchase something such as *SAP.* With a package such as *SAP,* there is less to negotiate between different ways to do things. Other lessons from the previous project included the need to co-locate people to work closely together to resolve conflicts, the need to proactively prevent burnout, the importance of explicit top-management support, and the key role that local areas must play in negotiating functionality. A positive aspect of the prior experience was that many team members had already experienced the problems with trying to create a global solution: differences in language, currency, and units of measure. Ultimately, the global order entry system was dismantled.

In March 1995, a group that had been chartered to look at *SAP* recommended to the board that the company buy it and implement it worldwide. A key motivator for going with a package rather than build it in-house was the increasing complexity of integrated solutions. In addition, many of the company's competitors and customers were implementing *SAP;* thus, as SAP develops more functionality, the company may find it difficult to keep up with competitors and do electronic commerce with their customers. The evaluating team found that *SAP* included about 80 percent of the company's legacy system functionality, with most of it at least as good, if not better, than the company's systems. While the company had built a set of integrated applications in the 1980s, newly purchased subsidiaries had never been brought into that set; *SAP* would enable their inclusion. Purchase would also enable further consolidation in Europe, for example, where the common market initiatives will provide tax incentives for such combinations. Moreover, it became obvious that it was impractical to maintain these systems and better to "get the leverage of using the capabilities of a company like *SAP* who could afford to pay thousands of programmers to keep their functionality up with best practice in the outside world" (head of IT in Europe).

The project team, initially formed in mid-1995, was charged with a companywide rollout of *SAP* by 2000. At first the team was highly motivated but overly optimistic and frustrated. There were no definitions of project goals or processes or agreement between the project leaders. In January 1996, the head of IT intervened to focus the group on a pilot with a hard deadline of July 1, 1996, and with a full implementation. A new project manager was appointed at that time.

In June 1996 the project team was restructured. One change was to replace the coordinators who had mainly a business background with people with more IT experience in order to prepare for implementation. Also at this time the team set the global implementation schedule, with priorities, to help focus it.

D. Realized and Anticipated Outcomes

In general, targeted implementation dates have been met. In October 1996, according to plan, *SAP* went live in three locations. A *location* is anything from a sales office to a major client. As of October 1998, the Enterprise solution has been implemented in over 80 percent of fifty-two targeted sites. The plan called for implementing *SAP* in all locations by the end of 1998. Currently, the project team expects to install *SAP* in most of the remaining locations by the end of 1998, although several small locations will be converted in the first quarter of 1999.

Once *SAP* is implemented globally, it will be the platform for identifying and realizing additional reengineering opportunities. In the IT brochure, ten reengineering opportunities have been identified for "immediate attention," with *reengineering* defined as a radical change that will bring between 25 and 50 percent improvement in one or more key process measures within two years. It is estimated that reengineering efforts will provide more than $.5 billion in savings or cost avoidance in a three-year period. Separate projects will be organized for each reengineering effort, and these projects will be resourced and managed by business processes.

III.   Deployment Strategies and Techniques

A. Methods and Processes

There was no existing methodology for implementing packaged software. In early 1996, a subgroup within the global team developed and refined a prototyping process from need identification to development to implementation. This process has iterations of analysis of desired functionality, design of functionality via prototyping workflows, and implementing of functionality. Most of the businesspeople find this too restrictive, but the technical people find it too loose and lacking in detail. The project planner thinks it is sufficient because of the extensive project experience of the team.

This methodology is evolving, and there were many modifications after the pilot implementation. The new process is not much larger but articulates things that can go wrong. There are standards for documentation that are "pretty much a deity," but other than that, they have worked in a fluid and flexible way. The process also deals with upgrades from *SAP* and anticipated legal changes, especially in Europe.

The Development and Implementation Process outline consists of activities/events of three types: *SAP* upgrades, Development, and Implementation, with specific activities/events that can trigger activities within and across types. Development activities include the following:

1. Functionality list and prioritization process.
2. Process development.

3. Global work flow review with global business process manager.
4. Intranet distribution.
5. Integration testing.
6. Controlled configuration.
7. Organizational structure and site and country configuration.
8. Area team training.

The primary analysis document, created as a Development activity, is the functionality list, which has about 200 to 300 items. This list includes all requests for functionality to be put into the system at different levels. It includes lower-level functions (e.g., define a bill of lading) as well as higher-level functions (e.g., a way to handle cash sales). The functional specifications come from the global team and local users. Sometimes this is done via phone or E-mail, but in some cases, especially in Asia, this is done by global team members visiting the local sites. One advantage of going on-site is that the global team members are better able to understand the legal and cultural business requirements of the site. Then the implementation leader on the global team maps the requests against what is currently available in *SAP* and identifies what is possible now and what can be reasonably added for initial implementation. That creates the functionality list for that site.

At intervals the list is grouped by the four process areas and prioritized, and the tasks required to produce that functionality are defined and assigned, with a deadline. Items get a high priority if they are needed for implementations that are scheduled to be done in the near future. What is most difficult is coming up with the estimates of effort needed to develop a functionality item. There are no benchmarks for this. Project managers use no tools but make estimates based on experience (which has become easier as they have implemented more).

There is also a separate plan for developing documentation. This documentation is based on the decomposition of the global work flows and is the only formal way of storing what has been learned from the project. To do this, the developers used PIDs (process and instrument diagrams). These show the work flow, how the flow goes in terms of how business is done, and the processes needed. The work flow decomposition was initially done by the global team members in light of the functionality of *SAP*, but with each implementation, members take the existing PID to the local users for review. In some cases, users requested additional subprocesses to meet local needs.

An early decision was made to not make modifications to *SAP*. (SAP does have hundreds of approved "user exits," which are specified places in the application where *SAP* guarantees the integrity of exiting and reentering *SAP* so that, for example, you can go out to an external device for collecting data.) There have in fact been a few (five to six) modifications at the company that have been made for global business reasons rather than for some site-specific needs. As one team member described it, "it takes an act of God, if you will, in this case the President and CEO, to actually approve those. It goes all the way up the ladder." The view has been "if the global process has to change we'll change it, put a modification into it and go forward with the modifications for everybody, not just one site" (global team implementation leader). These are not significant modifications, just a few lines of code in some cases.

B. Rollout Strategies

Implementation activities include the following:

1. Functional scope analysis
2. Site power user training
3. Data migration
4. Work flow validation testing
5. End-user training
6. Implementation and startup

The choice of the pilot location was based on finding a relatively remote site that was at the end of the supply chain but multisite and able to implement the whole array of functionality. By selecting a pilot that was at the end of the supply chain, there was less interference with the legacy systems. Since a location at the end is mostly receiving data, it isn't generating many data (which if wrong would ripple through many sites).

Subsequent site selection is based on definable locations that can be brought up together. Implementations are both pushed and pulled. Initially, corporate and IT leadership pushed the project. Because there have been more implementations, there is pull from sites that see the benefits and see that top management is serious about the project. The project manager remarked:

> It's kind of like this is a big freight train, it gets faster every day. So you've got one of two choices: you get on or you get run over. You either will be a part of the process or a victim.

Members from the global and local area teams created the implementation schedule. There is an attempt to match implementation dates with the dates when needed functionality will be ready. If they don't match, however, then the global and local area teams decide whether to change the implementation date or temporarily eliminate some functionality. If they cannot decide, the decision is escalated up to the process managers (so far, occasionally) and then to the process directors (so far, once). To date, the teams have made every implementation deadline but have not eliminated critical functionality.

Implementation at sites is done by the area implementation team and coordinated by the implementation manager from the global team. About a month before implementation, the team prepares a detailed plan of the final two or three weeks of tasks since implementation is "an instantaneous flip of the switch." This planning includes training; data cleanup and loading; identifying cutover tasks; and testing each piece of hardware, infrastructure, and the configuration. The plan for data articulates what data, in what sequence, need to be entered. The global team members map the data from the legacy systems onto the new *SAP* format, transfer and edit the data, and set up the system for subsequent data entry. That data set is then used in training the local users and to assess the impact on work. The production data are then loaded.

C. Training, Maintenance, and Support Strategies

The training strategy distinguishes between *conceptual education,* which addresses the "big picture" of the Enterprise solution and the global changes in business process work flows, and *transactional training,* which focuses on the use of *SAP* for a task. The latter is based on task groupings identified in the work flow decompositions prepared as part of systems analysis. There are also some training modules on general topics, such as "What Is *SAP?*"

A special training facility is used to transfer knowledge from the global project team to the area implementation teams and power users. This training starts at the very conceptual level and drills down to the details of system operation. There is a variety of courses, and so training at the facility can last from between one and one-half to six weeks.

The training that end users receive is based on a role mapping of each's tasks against the functions of *SAP* implemented at that site. The central training plan does not address any job changes or expansion, which are dealt with at the local site; that is, it is the local site management's decision to change jobs as enabled by *SAP* or to keep all jobs as they were prior to *SAP*. Currently, there are about one hundred different training courses.

Local users are trained by the area team and the power users, on-site, as well as by using computer-based training purchased from a vendor that translates the training material into multiple languages. The company also plans to use the train-the-trainers approach at larger sites. This is an area of concern for some, since the number of people will increase quickly (from less than a thousand people knowing *SAP* to thousands in twelve months). "The sheer volume of numbers scare me" (global training coordinator). The number of trainers needed far exceeds the number of area team members, and so additional help and classrooms will be needed for training.

Current efforts are focused on developing the maintenance structure, called the "business process steward structure." This will be part of the "global process network" within IT, which is made up of people around the world who are charged with making processes more effective. This group will be formed with some people from the global team and some who were not on the project. The goal is to have a blend of project knowledge, IT skills, and business processes. This group will be responsible for new releases of *SAP*.

Ongoing user support is provided by a local help desk, which tries to resolve problems with local power users. There is also an "escalation" process by which problems not resolved locally are sent to corporate IT and then, if needed, to *SAP*.

IV.   Challenges and Resolutions
A. Selling the Solution
There is a concerted effort to motivate the need for change and to actively sell the solution. Top managers recognize that a critical success factor missing from the earlier global order entry system project was explicit, broad-based top-management support. That support is clearly evident in the Enterprise solution. Top managers are not only active in selling the solution and in funding it but also signed a letter stating that the Enterprise solution is the number 1 initiative for the company. One global process coordinator uses this letter as a "letter of introduction so that if anyone gives me flack, this is what our corporate heads have said we were going to do next year. And, I'm trying to do it, so, 'Are you going to help me, yes or no?'"

The need for the change (in both the *SAP* platform and the global supply chain) is communicated by the CEO and the head of IT:

> Our top management in the area . . . regularly stand or sit in front of groups of employees and explain the need to do all this stuff. What it means, what it is, why we need to do it, what it's going to mean for the organization. And that has all been done with a very consistent message in a very open way right from day one. And I think that gives employees confidence that there is nothing being kept from them. And, so they're prepared to support and go along with this as it plays out because of course we had to say right from the word go, "Well, we don't know exactly what this is going to look like, but this is the big picture." But our senior management have put a lot of time and effort into that and I think it has paid off.

Helping this communication is the fact that the new head of corporate IT is much more visible that the previous head, and so IT and the Enterprise solution are much more visible.

Mechanisms used to sell the solution include brochures, internal house communications, forums held by leaders at various levels, and just talking with people at various locations to explain the vision and the project. Initially, this was clearly top-down communications. On an ongoing basis, the head of IT makes progress reports to the operating committee and to the IT organization (on a six-week basis).

Part of selling the solution is getting people comfortable with the fact that they will be revisiting *SAP* work flows and software on a continuous basis. This contrasts with the past mentality of project teams and users, which was that systems are built to last for twenty-five years and therefore they must be perfect to begin.

B. Managing Changes to Technology and Business Processes
The general climate for change was described by the project managers as "probably better than most places, but still difficult," in that the company has always had an open culture with lots of both vertical and horizontal communications and with the freedom to disagree and debate openly. However, one coordinator describes the company as being consensus minded in that it does not like conflict, and therefore employees strive to avoid conflict. This led to large differences in how things were done in the various locations around the world.

While the general climate for change was relatively good, this project represented a big change for the company. Moreover, everyone thinks his or her processes are different and unique, and getting everyone to adopt common global processes is not easy. Ultimately, everyone must conform. The project manager explains that everyone must "participate in the process or be a victim . . . it's kind of like binary." The head of IT in Europe thinks that success depends on local managers' "commitment and enthusiasm":

> If you've got local management, the employees trust their local managers. I think people who turn up from that [corporate] office, however nice and well spoken and all of that, they're still not the people that employees were with day in and day out.

In Europe there has been a range of local commitment to the solution. In some sites the problem comes from the fact that the sites were once separate companies that were acquired five to seven years ago but allowed to operate autonomously. The *SAP R/3* implementation for those sites represents the first time they have been asked to conform to company practices, and so it is very deep change. Where there is not the local support and enthusiasm, the sites use the "change workshops" or "change management meetings."

Change Management Techniques. A key change management technique employed for this solution was a series of change management meetings. The meetings last an entire day and include the area business sponsors, the area implementation leader and some team members, and the entire site management and site team. The meetings are facilitated by a person from human resources. This is the time for local managers to discuss their concerns and expectations, and for team representatives to clarify roles and responsibilities, and for the whole group to engage in some team building. The European head of IT explained:

> Lock them in a large room and get into really smashing out what is it we're doing, what's the scope of this thing, and what kind of contract should we have between each of those three groups so that everyone can walk out of the room and know who's doing what, why they are doing it, how they're going to do it, and what is expected of each group by each other group.

Once all the issues are raised, the participants go into contracting mode in which the project leader and team commit to meeting agreed-upon expectations. Key to this is a kind of "bonding" among the sponsors, the sites, and the area team. Conflicts are raised, often by local managers who feel that the global solution will not work for them because of unique needs. Here the business sponsors and team members use their influencing skills as well as argue that this is what it means to become global. At this point, participants realize that being global requires concrete and sometimes radical changes in the way things are done. Techniques such as these meetings and other communications help the local sites work through the "shock of reality."

There are occasions when contracting is truly a two-way street. In at least one case, the area implementation team had to go back to the global team and push it to change some functionality, since in the change management meeting the team had been agreed that some local functionality was essential to serve the customers. "So, it isn't just carrot and stick by the sponsors with the local management. There is a genuine contract that they will get what they need to continue doing their business."

Following up on these general meetings, the implementation manager from the global team takes the local management through the specific work flows and the changes required at a very specific level. Sometimes there is open resistance, despite the fact that the teams have a contract, and the implementation team is not treated very well at the site. In these cases, the problem is sent to higher management (both business and IT). Higher management forms a kind of "war council" to meet with local management as well as their bosses and the process sponsors, put the issues on the table, and communicate the mandate. The business sponsors now know that this is part of their leadership. If there is not strong leadership at a site, the carrot approach won't work and a big stick will be needed.

Human Resources Role. The human resources area is also involved in this change effort. Its role is to prepare people for changes with the new work design. HR people are taking the strategy of putting in the new work flow first, followed closely by training and education around how to redesign the work. HR people feel they need to show employees the change, and then it is real and they can react to it. In sites already implemented, there have been job changes. For example, the customer service people now need to do more than just take orders, including assuming some roles formerly performed by credit management people. This change has caused some negative reactions and some turnover from those people who did not want to get out of their little boxes and did not think about the change as job enrichment or how it was helping the company.

Impact of Change. The global implementation manager commented that the changes sometimes appear "huge" to employees before implementation, but afterwards, they realize they are doing the same basic transactions, just in a different way. The larger difference is the fact that the system is totally integrated and requires data discipline not previously required to use it. The project manager noted that "discipline has not been one of our strong suits, culturally. . . . But we're learning that if you don't execute with a certain level of discipline, you pay the price later." He says the software requires such discipline because a global integrated system is unforgiving; once you implement it, "when you push the go button, that baby blows all over the world, right now. And to get it back is one heck of a painful process."

C. Controlling and Coordinating the Process

Team motivation and cohesion have been built and maintained in several ways. During a week-long kickoff meeting for the global team, upper management spoke, mission statements were developed, the values of the team were clarified, and team-building exercises were conducted. Team members were told, "Leave your area hats outside the door. We're in here now as a global team." In breakout sessions, team members talked about direction for the project, how to work as a team, and how to pick teammates.

Efforts to maintain control and motivation continued as the project progressed. The team has social events that included spouses. On Fridays, 30 to 40 percent of the team members wear their Enterprise solution shirts with the project logo. Team members have satchels with the same logo. Periodically there are Enterprise Solution meetings, which may focus on communication about project status or team motivation. For example, the head of IT has spoken to the team to help manage its expectations about motivation, with a graph showing how motivation can shift over time, and about ways to even out and prevent extreme highs and lows. At times, meeting focus is on evaluating the project process and what needs to be changed. Such meetings are held two or three times a year and serve to remotivate as well as communicate project information.

A prime source of motivation for some is the work itself. By continuing to develop functionality that they haven't done before and continuing to implement in new sites, they keep the work fresh and challenging. According to one team member, another motivating factor is that "people want it to succeed. People understand that we're looking at a fundamental change in the company, the way it's going to run." Even now, with an aggressive implementation schedule, he thinks that "that's what's keeping people going at the moment."

Performance evaluations and merit increases are clearly tied to performance on the project, including evaluations from peers and supervisors. The people who were selected for the project were already high performers, and now they have to exceed that level to be recognized. Despite the fact that many team members have developed expertise that would command high salaries in the market, people have not left, and the company has not raised salaries a great deal. Most believe that the location and family commitments to the area keep people from leaving. Two people believe management purposely selected people they thought were so tied to the area they would not be easily "lured away by consultants for the big money."

Coordinating individual efforts is done informally on a task-by-task basis. Before the pilot implementation, people were pulled into workshops to work on specific functionality pieces. Afterwards there was no time for workshops, but people knew each other and where the "touch points" are between processes and functions—where different parts affect one another.

One coordinator described how he monitored work on his team by walking around and informally discussing things with people (he calls it "rounds"). He expects team members to solve their own problems; since they have the expertise and have been working with the details, he does not "quarterback from an easy chair" with them. There are no status reports made at set intervals (daily, weekly, and monthly). As coordinator, he provides the project manager a bulleted list of accomplishments monthly and talks with him on an ongoing basis. Another process coordinator was unhappy with the lack of meetings for the entire subteam and with the difficulties in using the phone or teleconferencing because of the few hours in which working days overlap.

When team members are assigned functions, they make task lists, broken down into specific activities (e.g., translate into French, test). There are differences in how technology-related tasks are accomplished. The process coordinators have IT resources assigned directly to them, but not all team members do. For example, the person in charge of documents uses influence to get the IT resources to complete some of these tasks. To reward these individuals, he praises them, informs their bosses about their efforts, and provides input into their annual reviews.

D. Working in a Global Environment

The project has required reorientation from an international to a global company. One global team member thinks that selecting a package that was designed and developed in Europe helped from the beginning to prevent a U.S.–centered feel to the project:

> [That] was a major impact for the U.S. folks. It was the first time they ever had to deal with documentation that wasn't all in English. And, you know, they're kicking along and all of a sudden they see German. And, they can't read and so they get frustrated. Well, that's the way the Europeans have being feeling for twenty-five years with our systems. So, there was an awakening for a lot of folks.

Moreover, the package is a kind of neutral third party so that the users don't feel like a corporate solution or a solution from one of the other areas is being forced on them.

One team member noted that it was critical to be together when discussing differences in law, business, and customs among countries and cultures; there is a need to see the other person, be able to draw pictures, to communicate less formally as well as nonverbally. A central location is also an advantage in recruiting people from the areas who view working in the United States, at corporate headquarters, as a good career move. At the same time, such a move is a disadvantage because some local sites are unwilling to move key people totally to the United States because they fear they will never get them back. Because of this problem of co-locating people, there is a general view that the project is understaffed. For example, one group leader is short five people.

This is the first project in which the company utilized a global–local area project team structure, and the global implementation manager thinks this has had a good impact. Individuals associated with different work flows and processes are talking with each other and through a single representative on the project teams, which has resulted in their agreement on common global processes and considering things in terms of process, not functional area. While the interactions leading to these outcomes were informal, these changes were anticipated and desired. What was not anticipated was the need to agree on very detailed items and that the process was not one grand meeting during which everything was decided but involved rather smaller, day-to-day decisions.

A great deal of conscious attention was given to preventing burnout in the project team because of the type of high-achieving people selected for the project (who might have a tendency this way) plus the acknowledgment that they were doing much with a few people as well as traveling a good deal for extended periods. Also, one team member of both global order entry system and the *SAP R/3* project team said the company burned out many people on the previous project, and so it learned that it needed to deal with the problem. Mechanisms used for preventing burnout included a diagnostic measure during initial team building to help people understand how to relax, making sure people take their vacations, and employing an outside counseling resource to help monitor stress. The focus is on identifying each individual's self-care techniques. One team member talked about discussing burnout within the group and trying to keep "telling each other what a good job we were doing, you know, rally the troops."

This concern for the worker is part of the company value system but it is also a recognition that if key members of the global team leave, the informal coordination currently being used will suffer. One coordinator argued that a prime reason for the team's good communication and coordination is that the team consists of experienced professionals—not just in their fields but with the company. "We've always worked well together . . . a lot of good personality mixes . . . we can joke, we can laugh." Respect is also voiced for the expertise and abilities of others. In fact, this mutual respect is something the whole company values, and it is the number 1 point in the project's operating principles on how to create a positive environment.

E. Addressing Cultural Differences

Differences in language, currency, and measures can all be points of conflict. With the language difference, the translated words on a document can cause confusion when they do not match or make inappropriate matches with the terms used in *SAP*. These conflicts are usually resolved via E-mail, occasionally by a teleconference. One problem for team members who are involved with many other subgroups is that they can be overloaded with phone calls and E-mail requests for help with problems or concerns, which can interfere with developing new functionality.

For the global team, the leader of the European area implementation team thinks there are still people who need training on how to deal with different cultures and different languages. One project manager feels that more training on differences would have led to speedier progress in understanding and communicating with one another. For example, the way in which decisions are made differ by region, with Asian cultures building consensus for a decision but European employees are comfortable with a hierarchical approach.

The European implementation team leader thinks it is important that team members understand the sometimes subtle cultural differences (e.g., in Germany, businesspeople are not addressed by their first names). She sees a substantive danger from team members not knowing the legal requirements of other countries, which might result in a problem if global standard procedures don't comply legally in certain countries. She cites the following as an example:

> In Europe it's legal to pay third party or distributors for when they get business. It's almost like a commission to them. But it's not explicit on an invoice. Now, that's the way they do those commissions. In the U.S. that's illegal. If there's a commission, it has to be known to the customer . . . to a point. . . . the folks in the U.S. were just aghast that you could do that. And, that's the way business is in Europe. And, all legitimate, all up-and-up.

F. Transferring Knowledge

The global team gained much knowledge from its experiences, including its mistakes. But the knowledge that it transfers to the area teams focuses on how the system works, not how it doesn't work. So it is difficult for the area teams to get to the level of understanding of the global team, and they don't always know the right questions to ask. Sometimes the global team goes on-site to help with implementations because of lack of local knowledge (or cooperation). As the area teams become more experienced, the amount of global team involvement lessens, and global efforts center mainly on data loading, troubleshooting, and work flow issues.

Formal knowledge transfer is accomplished by the specialized training. Area teams and power users are trained on the system's functionality and configuration. The only formal way in which team members' learning about cultures is transferred to others is via job shadowing.

G. Moving from the Pilot to a Large-Scale Implementation

There is a general recognition that the difference between the pilot implementation and full-scale implementations is massive. The project team members prepared themselves for this transition. In particular, after the pilot, a meeting was held to document lessons learned from the pilot. Members' homework was to bring to the meeting specifics they had learned on Post-it notes so that they could be easily put up, grouped by topics, and shared with others.

In addition, the project team made changes to how the project was carried out after the pilot. One specific change concerned project planning, which was not done in detail for the pilot. Rather, only task-level milestones and due dates were in place (e.g., final op testing done, testing for materials). A conscious decision was made not to add the overhead of detailed planning, which, from the view of one team member, reflected the fact that many of the project leaders during the pilot were more visionaries than detailed project managers. There has been a shift and, according to this team member, "the fields have been sown and we need to just raise the crop. So, the emphasis on detail has changed." This is especially necessary as the project teams start doing multiple implementations concurrently. One leader thinks the tasks are still not detailed enough (they are at the level of thirty to forty hours). The project planner has a continuing concern that the lack of detail and the estimating difficulties have resulted in overloaded team members.

H. Measuring Success

Ultimate project responsibility rests with the CEO and the head of IT. Implementation success means meeting schedule and functionality commitments. An Optimization leader assesses a site's progress by measuring and monitoring the site against a milestone plan:

> Milestone A—change management in place.
> Milestone B—implementation planning, training, and related activities accomplished.
> Milestone C—actual implementation in the site.
> Milestone D—site is stabilized (people are comfortable and there is no change in
>   performance level).
> Milestone E—productivity gains realized from the Enterprise solution and reengineering.

Specific measures of success include comfort in use, number of times users ask for help, number of workarounds in place, maintenance of data discipline task performance, amount of overtime, and number of customer complaints. The project team has developed a questionnaire to be completed immediately after implementation as well as a few months after.

Currently no site has achieved milestone E, but one Japanese site and the European sites are at milestone D. Some sites are successful, some are struggling (in one case because a decision was made to move some business volume to a location without adding people at the same time *SAP* was implemented).

The ultimate success of the solution will be measured over a longer time frame than implementation, based on the impact on the processes. They company is in the process of developing measures around core components of customer service, cycle time, quality, and productivity. Each business process will be measured for effectiveness on each of these four components. An example of a process measure is to look at the product delivery process and to measure the time it takes from entering an order to its shipping date—the cycle time, as well as the time for all the subprocesses in between. This is "an interesting challenge . . . so we're struggling a little bit with that" (IT head).

The METRICS Solution

I.   Background

The Metrics solution was conceived by a multibillion-dollar technology firm founded in the 1930s. Today, the company has a range of products that generally falls into one of three categories: measurement, computing, and communications. This company employs over 114,000 people worldwide, with sales, manufacturing, and R&D facilities in more than 40 countries and sales and support offices and distributorships in more than 120 countries.

The culture at the company is entrepreneurial, and innovative behavior is encouraged and rewarded. Local autonomy, expertise, and management are the norm. Working relationships tend to be team oriented rather than hierarchical, and the company is frequently cited as among the best places to work. Communication is very open, and at least one manager believed the lack of a formal bureaucracy is critical to success since many of the company's competitors are small and quite agile.

The company's operations are grouped into three main regions: Asia-Pacific, Europe, and the Americas. In each of these regions are six major organizations, one of which is the Computer organization. The Computer organization accounts for the majority of the company's business. Major products of the Computer organization include multiuser systems, servers, workstations, professional services, RISC technology, object technology, and telecommunications solutions. A large and fast-growing segment of this organization is the customer support business unit, which contracts with customers of the company's products to provide varying levels of service. Two critical aspects of providing contracted service are to be able to evaluate the quality and speed of service and to understand the costs and time required for servicing various products. The Metrics solution was undertaken in the customer support business unit and focuses on providing timely information on hardware repair.

A. Information Technology and Information Management
This company has a centralized IT group that provides traditional information technology services and support within the company. About four years ago, there was a "pull" from the business side of the Computer organization to create a formal and separate Information Management (IM) organization. The goal was to have a unit own the actual strategies for, as well as tactics for the deployment and delivery of, the IM solution. The business users demanded an information-based unit that would proactively help the businesses use technology to meet the needs of the business units; the IT organization was seen largely as a unit to develop and support infrastructure. While the businesses recognized the value of the IT organization, they also looked to IM to "create the management of the data and the process, the connection with the business, the understanding of the business" (senior IT manager).

Thus, the formal IM organization was born, and the Metrics solution was its responsibility. The goal of the Information Management Program is to help customer support decision makers by providing easy-to-access, understandable information and knowledge about the customer support businesses. Systems such as the Metrics solution are being developed to help business users gain insights into the company's businesses. This understanding will form the basis for business innovation, including recognition of new business opportunities, business inefficiencies, and business threats (Intranet page, 1997).

II.   Solution and Project Description
A. The Project: Goals, Objectives, and Drivers
The primary business purpose of the Metrics solution is to provide an information management database for operational and tactical repair delivery data for use in decision making with regard to the hardware repair delivery part of the customer support business. To develop the Metrics solution, IM worked with managers throughout the world to establish a core set of hardware repair metrics and gain agreement on the definition and calculation of those metrics. The Metrics solution provides local and regional managers as well as corporate analysts with data on hardware repair that is based on "the same logic applied to the same data source" (Intranet page, 1997). The Metrics solution is a data warehouse built using Red Brick technology.

The primary user community is made up of the business information managers and their IM providers who are part of the customer support business unit. In particular, the manager of service delivery engineering is one of two executive sponsors of the Metrics solution. The primary data content is repairs and inventory data. According to the Project Charter document (1996), key goals include the following:

- Implement hardware repair metrics (business solution measures) for call qualification and repair deliveries.
- Implement a flexible and timely information management architecture (a data warehouse) that can react rapidly to business change.
- Provide detailed data to allow operational and tactical reporting.
- Provide the standardization of reporting measures across headquarters and field operations.

B. Project History

The project to deploy the Metrics solution began in 1995. It followed a failed project that had attempted to standardize the way in which certain indicators (e.g., engineers' responsiveness to customers) were measured. The general approach of the failed project was to identify a set of metrics and have each country pick the ones it thought were relevant. While the countries may have implemented a common set of metrics, the standardization effort failed; if a country did not agree with the definition of the metric, it simply coded around the standard definition. This older system, therefore, was not particularly useful for global management because of all of the different regional definitions and interpretations of the metrics data. When this system was in place, considerable time was spent in multigeography meetings discussing differences in data rather than discussing the real problems indicated by the data. It was difficult to move beyond the "whose data are right" issue.

In the last several years, there has been a strategy shift to more standardization, and headquarters is assuming more global responsibility for certain business processes. In addition, from an IT point of view, the company is beginning to replace legacy systems with enterprisewide applications (e.g., *SAP R/3*), which also demand more standardization across locations. Moreover, the key business managers are known for being "metrics driven," and they pushed hard for standardization in the hardware support delivery area. During this same time period, the business managers associated with support delivery had gone through a round of manual planning that revealed a problem of understanding the hardware repair business on a global basis. The managers recognized a real need for data on which they could all agree.

While this recognition led to sponsorship from worldwide general management for global data on hardware metrics, the worldwide managers also knew that what was needed for headquarters would not exactly match the needs of the local regions. Thus, "the Big 9" countries (the nine countries in which the company has operations) were identified to participate in the project, especially the early phase of determining specific requirements (i.e., hardware metrics). These countries were identified based on their share of the worldwide business (i.e., high-volume countries) and their involvement in other active projects within the community. Each country then selected a representative to participate in the Metrics solution project. A partnership developed between IM, which had the technology to build a system, and the business managers who had a felt need for the data.

C. The Project Team

Requirements definition was performed on a worldwide basis. The core project team is distributed with development teams in the United States and in the United Kingdom. The core team, which included business, IT, and IM representatives, met in the United States or the United Kingdom about every three months for three- to four-day meetings. Between these face-to-face meetings, the core team would have one- to two-hour teleconferences. Some of the core project members worked on the project full time, but most of the members who were process owners also had other on-going responsibilities. While some core team members had worked together before, many were people new to the team and the job. No formal team building was done, nor was any attempt made to provide a separate team identity.

The U.K. team consists of eight to ten members. There are also implementation teams for the different regions consisting of people from the local regions and from headquarters. The local representatives are largely responsible for coordinating tasks to ensure that all tasks happen. Training is also done with both worldwide and local people. The local representatives are responsible for getting the right people in the room, and the worldwide people actually do the training.

A team of people is also in place (twelve analysts, plus three or four contractors) that uses the baseline warehouse to build specific solutions to answer very specific business questions. The role of this group is to determine the needs of the field operations (Europe, the Americas, and Asia/Pacific) and to combine those needs with an overall global business perspective to build an effective solution. This group is also responsible for supporting the local users (about 50); it is part of the IT organization.

D. Project Outcomes

Project objectives have been developed and documented in the Project Charter (1996). For each objective, specific measures are also articulated, for example

Objective	Measure
Provide business solution for measurement and reporting of worldwide hardware repair delivery service metrics.	Produce business solution on a timely basis that is accessible by local field operation and worldwide business users.
Implement same name measures across geographies.	Adopt same name metrics by field operations.

Specific project deliverables and completion criteria are also documented in the Project Charter (1996), for example

Project Deliverable	Completion Criteria
Project Charter	Approval and sign-off by sponsors.
Standardization of metrics for coding in support of hardware delivery metrics.	Adoption of standardized coding structures by Big 9 countries.
Field installation of architecture.	Successful alpha test and production implementation. User acceptance and sign-off.
Business view containing the primary fourteen hardware repair delivery metrics.	Worldwide agreement on delivery metrics definitions and specs included in software release.
Limited solution training.	Classes held and satisfaction from users with respect to the training received.

Besides these objectives and deliverables, project team members indicated the importance of meeting project budget and schedule targets. The team members feel that the business managers expect results in three to six months. At this company, in the schedule-budget-scope triangle of trade-offs, scope is always the victim. The senior IT manager noted that the budget is usually fixed, "there's incredible pressure on the timeline," and that the culture is "speed, speed, speed."

The senior IT manager feels that the Metrics solution is "getting successful," that momentum for people to switch from their old systems to the new solution is increasing. One important measure of success is that there is centralized access to consistent metrics data on a timely basis. Monthly data are available by the third working day of the next month in the worldwide data warehouse, and regional data are updated daily. The interface allows users to see the metadata; for each data element, they can access the definition of the element and its calculation logic. The perspective of a quality consultant user at headquarters is as follows:

> In terms of what I'm doing, it's just helped us understand a little bit more about the relationships between some of these performance variables. . . . I think a lot of the benefit really is coming . . . to our financial folks. They had very limited means to understand what the costs were for a lot of these delivery processes. Now with the advent of this solution, we really understand our costs a lot better. And I think that's really helped us drive some, not necessarily performance-related strategies, but some cost-related strategies that are allowing us to change our delivery metrics, because that's going to be a critical success factor for our future.

In addition, the Metrics solution was used for planning how many engineers were needed in each district in 1998. The plan was completed in two days, and, according to the quality consultant, the planners reported that "if they hadn't had the standardized centralized place to go for that, it would have taken them weeks and they would have been comparing apples and oranges."

III.   Deployment Strategies and Techniques
A. Methods & Processes
Forge Agreement on Common Processes. The first step of the process was to identify the set of hardware metrics for which data would be collected globally. Once the metrics were identified, the second step involved developing a common definition and calculation for each metric. To accomplish these critical first steps, a three-day face-to-face meeting was held in London. The business program manager was responsible for this phase of the project and coordinated this activity. The participants in this meeting included the representatives from the Big 9 countries and from worldwide headquarters.

Because of the support and sponsorship of the worldwide managers, the meeting participants came with the belief that there was a need for worldwide data and reporting. All representatives also came to the meeting with a list of metrics that they currently used to measure hardware service. In total, eighty to ninety metrics were identified. These metrics were cataloged and prioritized. The prioritization was relatively straightforward. Many were similar conceptually, even though some of these seemingly similar metrics were measured differently. There was therefore some consistency across managers with respect to which metrics were important but no prior agreement on how to measure and calculate them.

The group then examined each metric, top-down, and discussed how each was currently measured. Many of the metrics were being measured eight or nine ways. The group discussed the best way to measure each. During this three-day meeting, the group was able to agree on definitions and calculations for the top eighteen to twenty metrics. In some cases, the metric was new and so agreement on a standard definition and calculation was fairly easy. However, in those cases where the same metric was being used and calculated differently by different regions, the discussion was often contentious. But the group was able to weigh the cost of standardizing the metric against the benefits. The costs were associated with change, and the more established the metric, the more difficult it was to change. A number of these tough decisions were put off. The process for coming to agreement was as follows:

- Identify the measure.
- Identify definitions and calculations.
- Present one calculation—put up one calculation as a catalyst for discussion and, in particular, to surface and verify assumptions related to the metric.
- Reach consensus.

For any follow-up discussion to clarify a meaning or assumption, the group tried teleconferencing but found the quality unacceptable and so used E-mail, which had two (more or less unanticipated) advantages: asynchronous communication and self-documenting. Two months later, the same group met again (face-to-face) to look at another set of metrics.

About halfway through the project, a feature was added to give easy worldwide access to standardized data and to reemphasize the power of standard data:

> You can go to this one web page and then do different reports against this information, by country or by product type, etc. So it really is consistent data throughout the whole world, a consistent way of measuring things. So, this wasn't something that was in the original project's specs, but it really came out, as we have to, just having the data standardized in the warehouse; you need a good way of presenting that and have people have access to that (senior IM manager).

Solution Development. Following the identification and definition of the metrics, the group gave a functional specification to the development team in the United Kingdom. The business program manager, responsible for eliciting business specifications, spent a week in the United Kingdom coordinating the work between the developers and managers and found that the developers needed more granular information from which to work: a data model and a technical specification. Primarily using E-mail, the business program manager communicated with the business managers and collected the necessary information. He then returned to the United Kingdom for four to five weeks to resolve issues. The business program manager felt that the face-to-face time with the developers, after the three-day meeting to determine business requirements, was essential. During this time of requirements uncertainty, the U.K. developers were developing the underlying architecture.

While there was some intention of locating development in the United States, there were not enough personnel available, so it was outsourced to the United Kingdom.. The U.S. team was supposed to manage the U.K. team's efforts remotely. For about six months, the development effort seemed to be repeating the "analysis–design–construction" loop. Eventually, a deliverable was released; however, major architectural problems were discovered. As a result, the solution was redesigned, and the extra time taken for development and the redesign caused the original 8-month project to become an 18-month project.

A complicating factor in the project was that the Metrics project was concurrent with work on a companywide data warehouse infrastructure project. According to one IM manager, this concurrency was intentional. He believes that most centralized data warehousing efforts are too large to implement big bang but rather should be done in phases. In each phase, part of the data warehouse infrastructure is built and some of the data sources are cleaned and standardized to support a needed business application. The business application, in this case the Metrics solution, provides the business push for the data warehouse effort that supports it.

The Metrics solution was the first to be built upon the new data warehouse environment. Prior to the new environment, applications were written to draw data directly from transaction processing systems, although there were some successful data warehouses and data marts in operation that were based on different technology platforms. In the new environment, data from around 200 source systems are pulled at set time intervals into three regional data warehouses and then into a central data warehouse. The Metrics solutions draws hardware repair data from this central data warehouse into its own database for processing. The solution will ultimately have more than 5,000 users worldwide, and the data warehouse currently uses about 14 gigabytes of data (of the estimated 250 gigabytes of data in the entire warehouse when completed).

B. Rollout Strategies
The Metrics solution will eventually be rolled out to 68 countries. At the time of this research, the status of the Metrics solution is as follows: (1) the data warehouse is implemented in each field operation and is the primary source of operational data for many local country operations, (2) the Phase I validation is in progress with country representatives, and (3) the project has good visibility. Phase II of the project is currently on hold pending stabilization of the underlying hardware and software architecture.

Phase I of the Metrics solution was implemented first in the Asia-Pacific area, then in Europe, and finally in the Americas. Because Asia-Pacific had no comparable existing system, it had a very large need for the new system. The Americas had their own system in place and were the most reluctant to implement the Metrics solution. Europe fell in between the two extremes.

The business program manager worked with a team in each country to reconcile the various data in preparation for the implementation of the Metrics solution. He made it clear that the project team and worldwide management wanted a credible reflection of the operations in each country. Along with the country teams, the business program manager
- Validated existing data sources.
- Asked if other data were needed.
- Examined inconsistent data for needed changes.
- Verified that the countries were using codes as agreed.

In most cases, local and central project team personnel were responsible for training the business users and the IT staff who support the solution locally. Local staff identified who needed training, and in most cases the training was delivered by the centralized project team members. One divisional IM manager preferred a second model for training in which the local field representatives come to the corporate location for two to three weeks to build expertise, and then they do the local training. He commented that these field representatives then became "the 'spreading of the good word' kind of person out among their own field ops and become the champion at that point for their worlds."

C. Maintenance and Support Strategies

Each region has its own data warehouse, and each region has added its own "bolt-ons." Local users are asked to justify bolt-ons by considering whether they are willing to incur the five-year costs of ownership: development, support, and change management. Local IT groups are not given source code, but the Red Brick technology enables them to create reference tables that are built around the core solution. At this point, there is not a clear strategy for dealing with long-term support and maintenance. The intent is that the local regions will support and maintain any changes that they have made. The reality at the company is that it is difficult to enforce one solution. According to one divisional IM manager,

> We'd lose credibility if we didn't provide an environment that both allows and encourages them to go out and do that [customize]. But there's that whole administrative support headache that nobody really wants to own up to and they want to kind of pretend that it doesn't exist until things start to break.

The company is still in the process of developing an appropriate way to route calls for support. While calls for IT-related problems should be handled by the local IT staff, concerns about the definition and calculation of metrics should be routed to the business managers in the division, perhaps escalating to corporate headquarters.

IV.   Challenges and Resolutions

A. Controlling and Coordinating the Process

Much of the control and coordination of this project was based on the use of informal techniques: relationships, prior history of people working together, consensus building, and team-based management and coordination (rather than strict hierarchical control). In fact, this project proceeded without ever naming one person to manage the project. At times, three or four people seemed to assume the role of project manager and, as one senior IM manager said, "at one point in time about eight people might have thought they were the project manager . . . it was multiple projects going on and kind of loosely tied together, but there was no real one defined person responsible for the whole." In part, this lack of formal structure is due to the culture of the company in which individuals are expected to work things out at a group or team level rather than going up through the hierarchy.

This lack of structure proved to be both effective and ineffective. Because of this lack of structure, there often was no clear communication between the groups but a perception that the project was less efficient than it could have been. The lack of communication was especially problematic, given the distributed nature of the project team. There is no requirement that individual teams working on the project produce status communications, although this was done in at least one case with a team Web site. As a result, much communication was done via personal point-to-point conversations and, of course in some cases, lack of knowledge led to redundant work.

This lack of structure was not a barrier in those instances when one person served in multiple roles. For example, the business program manager was part of several "subteams" and found that he acted as a conduit among those teams. Also, one of the senior IM managers had a good prior relationship with the main business sponsor, and when problems escalated, they were able to jointly resolve the problems.

Despite the lack of a clear leader, individual team member commitment to the project was high. One process manager in IM believes that "what got us through this project was just everybody's individual commitment to it." The senior IS manager had specific suggestions for keeping the team members motivated and focused: Celebrate victories as they come but keep moving forward, institute a very strong input process in which people feel free to communicate ideas, and select people who are enthusiastic and who like challenges. One factor in the high motivation on the business side was the felt frustration in not having access to data needed to effectively run the business; a key factor for others was their belief that IM was the right mechanism to provide that information.

B. Working in a Global Environment

The early meetings in which metrics were articulated and defined were described by a business program manager as "organized chaos, grueling, painful." He commented that the many different cultures in the room made it difficult to communicate, but that it was critical to give everyone a voice. He found that the use of strong, key, and influential people in the meetings overcame this potential problem because they all seemed willing to participate. The business program manager was especially concerned that the representatives from some cultures would not participate in such a meeting and was glad that some locations were represented by someone from another culture who freely spoke up. Subsequently, the business program manager also used E-mail to communicate with some regions because he felt it was a better mode of communication for them.

The project team for the Metrics solution is quite global; many members are not native Americans, and the core development team is in the United Kingdom. The global nature of the team seemed to mitigate many problems typically reported by other nonglobal project teams working on this type of project.

C. Implementing Change

The main change for business users of the Metrics solution was to conform to a common solution and data definition; the challenge was to get all locations to accept the single solution. This was a change for all locations, since the company is rather decentralized, and it is a new "mind set" to have "the ability to share tools and an infrastructure, instead of having their own" (senior IT manager). The magnitude of this change differed by location. For a few locations, the changes were not onerous because they didn't have a high-volume business. Other locations had done a lot with metrics and were less willing to accept different ways of working with metrics. The senior IT manager observed, "What happens really is that some have to regress for others to progress, . . . and very often the one who you want to join the team is the one you want to learn from."

The business program manager commented that it was sometimes easy and sometimes difficult to enforce the use of standard codes. Even after the initial agreements by representatives, when local managers saw that they would be evaluated on the metrics and that in some cases the new calculations were not favorable to their operation, they tried to back out. As one senior IM manager described it, when the reports are produced and show that you only met your customer's commitments 93 percent of the time. That not only gets people's attention, and so the first thing they do is say, "Well I don't agree with the way you calculated that." So there was a lot of work again.

The work to regain agreement included reminding managers of their earlier agreement to the metrics in the meetings and, in some cases, escalation of the issue to higher management for resolution. In general, when managers encountered difficulties, they did the following to obtain a common solution:

- Reiterated the general principles at work in the case of metrics.
- Asked whether the general principles support the variation in use by the region.
- Reviewed the costs associated with lack of consistency.
- Explained the limits of development and why development could not handle the variations that were sometimes requested.

A strategy for reducing resistance to change was to involve, from the beginning, the professional users of the solution. Professional users use the solution "on the job, day in and out, this is their job, to really pull information, do the underlying analysis, and also some reporting." The IM management involves these professional users in designing change, establishing priorities for deployment, and selection of tools. "So that's a way to, on a worldwide basis, to really try and bring people into actually making the change, instead of having to just be submitted to the change" (senior IT manager).

D. Implementing the Metrics Solution
The senior IT manager noted that it was not always easy to determine the order of implementation, especially when many regions are clamoring for the new system. In general, implementation is most difficult at the region with its own highly developed system and procedures, which, in this case, was the Americas region. Thus, this region was at the bottom of the list. On the other hand, implementation is easiest where the need is greatest. For this project, the greatest need was in the Asia-Pacific region, which was where the Metrics solution was first implemented.

At each implementation site, local buy in was built with key personnel at that site. Implementers identified the one or two key people at the site whose evaluations would be trusted by others. Then they validated the solution with these "trusted advisors"; they ran reports with the old and the new system and then explained all the details of any differences and why the new information was better. This was a lengthy process, and "sometimes it would take longer than others . . . the Americas was harder again . . . it was just through perseverance and stubbornness, I guess that we're here. We didn't go away" (senior IM manager).

E. Dealing with Technology Issues
While the company has experience with data warehouses, it had not used this particular product (Red Brick), nor had it implemented a warehouse of such magnitude in terms of scope of change and number of sources. As a result, the company ran into several problems, most notably implementing before it had done a thorough requirements analysis, resulting in at least a three-month delay (see earlier section on *Methods and Processes*). The vendor told them they were not designing the warehouse correctly but were still creating a straight relational design. Although analysts from the vendor tried to tune the database and did make a lot of improvements, the company still needed to do significant rethinking and redesign.

Another technology issue arose that was outside their control but was typical of the problems of integrating separate systems, both in-house and purchased, over time. For example, an in-house tool was being used for access to legacy systems, while *Brio* was planned to be the data warehouse access tool. When the in-house access tool became a burning platform because it could not work with the new version of the operating system, *Brio* had to be implemented to work not just with the Metrics solution but also the legacy systems.

The CREDIT Solution

I.   Background

The Credit solution is being deployed by one of the largest banks in the world. Having recently merged with another large financial institution, this company employs around 70,000 people worldwide with operations in more than 50 countries. The new company employs a matrix management type of organizational structure and governance. At the time of the case study, the effects of the merger were still being felt by the employees, who were trying to merge the business processes and technology services of the two banks.

The developers and users of the Credit solution are part of the Global Trade Finance (also called Trade) organization. The Global Trade Finance organization has some business as well as technology responsibilities.

A. Information Technology Services

The structure and location of the IS organizations within the company were undergoing considerable change as a result of the merger. Historically, within the company, each business had its own IT organization that built systems, but the software and hardware infrastructure was centrally managed and maintained. Within its merger partner, each business had its own IT organization that both developed systems and managed its infrastructure; each business was also responsible for the long-term maintenance of its IT portfolio of software and hardware.

In the United States, the bank employs over 7,000 people in information systems. Most development activity occurs in this country, and funding for systems development outside the United States is less significant. The second largest IS shop, in the United Kingdom, employs around 200 people.

At the time of the case study, there were both centralized and decentralized IS organizations in place. As a newly created organization, the bank is struggling with the degree to which IT services will be centralized. At this point, the centralized support for infrastructure and support still exists. However, the Trade organization now has its own LAN support because the LAN support group came from the merger partner's organization.

II.   Solution and Project Description

A. The Project: Goals, Objectives, and Drivers

The Credit solution is intended to support letters-of-credit processing. This business, historically, has been viewed regionally. Many of the business drivers for the project came from the Asia region; it is the biggest market plus the biggest geography. The other regions (Europe and North America) were not driving the project as much, from a business point of view. Europe is a smaller market, although the Eastern European countries represent some growth. Europe is also a much smaller geographic area. For all intents and purposes, "North America" is New York, the center of all North American business. Besides the business opportunities and growth found in Asia, that region presented the greatest technological challenge due to the existing disparate systems built on hardware platforms that could no longer be supported.

The Credit solution has a multitiered user group. The primary end users are the internal bank operations personnel who support the business. Secondarily, management and sales personnel use the management information coming from the system. In addition, external bank customers of the letter-of-credit process have a link into the system and use the customer access pieces. There are about 550 users in North America, 250 in Asia, and 100 in Europe.

B. Project History

Trade Finance, including letter of credit, has historically been the "bread and butter of banking" although never a highly profitable or visible activity. Consequently, the technology to support letters of credit has largely been ignored. The existing systems are approximately twenty years old and have been patched numerous times over the years. Moreover, there is no one existing system but a range of systems developed for different technology platforms. In Asia, for example, there is a WANG system, but instead of having one WANG system maintained centrally, nine countries in Asia received a copy of the WANG software and subsequently modified it. A mainframe application is in use in Europe, and New York uses a DEC VAX system.

Over time, the IT organization recognized that if a global system existed, not only would all locations utilize the same hardware and software, but also the bank's customers would have a standard way to access the bank's products. In the period 1992 to 1993, a series of discussions was held to determine the standard architecture for the system. These discussions included both IS and business people; in the premerger company environment, both groups of people reported through the same structure, and so both were included in the discussion. However, according to the senior IS manager, the businesspeople saw this as a technology problem and solution and did not recognize the opportunity for reengineering the business process:

> They didn't fully understand that there was a business process reengineering effort that should have happened first, until the design and the definition of the system were well underway. Then somebody said, "But, gee, I don't do it this way," and "I don't do it this way," and "Why do we want to build it like this?" That building of consensus started waking some people up. . . . [But] the system was well underway before people realized the need for business process reengineering.

Possible solutions from external vendors were considered as well as the existing European mainframe solution. However, due to the need for a scalable solution (e.g., some locations have two people; others have 100) and for flexibility, the decision was made to build a customized solution using client/server technology.

Consensus Building. The consensus-building process really started about two years prior to the official start of the Credit solution, and it is still ongoing as enhancements are made to the application. The process involved a series of meetings with the same participants: division executives, regional representation from each location, technology representative, and local technology people. From an IT standpoint, the regions did eventually come to consensus on "being global." One of the carrots was the location of the development activity. The decision was made to develop the Credit solution in Hong Kong with project management in New York.

To determine initial specifications for the Credit solution, a group of managers went around the world, looking at different company systems as well as vendor offerings. The Analysis/QA manager of the Credit solution was part of this group; during this time (early 1990s), he was an operations manager in the Trade division. The business managers, who are responsible for revenues, realized they needed to work together to try to market customers effectively. To do this, a standardized system was required. The company has operations in thirty-one countries, and almost each country had its own system. The group (which included operations managers from the three regions: United Kingdom, New York, and Asia) examined how letters of credit were processed by different regions around the globe, and standardized the process. The operations managers said, "Well, maybe you have something better than us. Maybe we'll take your system and work around it to make sure that it is globalized." So they looked at all existing systems, clearly documenting their strengths and deficiencies and areas of improvements, and estimated what it would cost to make the system global. They then wrote a functional specification on the process, which they sent back to everyone for approval.

Reaching consensus was difficult, although the Analysis/QA manager noted that everyone agreed to the need for a global system "to enhance our ability to provide customer service and make sure we deliver what the customer needs." With the current disparate systems there was little ability to get information on a global basis. The Analysis/QA manager commented that people seemed to realize that the bank needed to move forward with this project or "be left behind." They saw the systems that other banks had in place and knew they were behind. Because of the costs of fixing any of the existing systems and due to lack of systems from vendors, plus the company's expertise with building global systems, the decision was made to build a system internally.

C. The Project Team
The core team is located in New York. Under the senior IS manager, there are several managers: the Analysis/QA manager, responsible for requirements analysis and quality control; the Systems Development manager, responsible for development; the Implementation manager, responsible for implementation; and the Training manager, responsible for training. In total, the senior IS manager has about 50 people reporting to her.

There is a large development group in Asia (about 15 or so people) who were originally responsible for the development of the global system but who are now responsible for interface development and conversion for Asia only. Another six people or so are located in the United Kingdom, doing the U.K. interface development and conversion. The senior IS manager's group in New York will handle the local requirements for the rest of Europe.

D. Project Outcomes
The Credit solution has been deployed in several countries in Asia, the United Kingdom, Germany, and the United States. The next implementations will be in the remaining locations in Europe.

Critical criteria of success are budget, schedule, and customer impact. Customer impact is measured, at least in part, by the number of customer phone calls about the system. Another success criteria is related to human resources, in particular, retaining and training staff.

III.   Deployment Strategies and Techniques

A. Methods and Processes

The intent is to have one version of the core system that is deployed everywhere. Currently, there are three versions of the system in existence; there are two locations that had to run older versions for an interim period of time. The hope is that these two locations will migrate to the supported version within a year.

A hub and satellite model is in place, in which central processing has been maintained on the system side. The hubs are the main processing locations (United Kingdom, Hong Kong, New York), and most of the technology sits in the hub locations. The satellites branch out around the hubs. The servers are regionalized with remote locations. Thus, the transactions are processed locally, but the data are sent into a regional location.

When the decision was made to move development from Hong Kong to New York, the Systems Development manager was brought to New York from the United Kingdom to form the core development team (there was no team at all in New York), to build up expertise in the Credit solution, and to take the application from its prior form (version 1) to version 2. The Systems Development manager's team has about 30 people. While the centralized team in New York is responsible for core development, the local teams build interfaces.

Version 1 is currently running production in Asia. The goal of version 2 is to rewrite the code from 16-bit to 32-bit technology; there were no functionality changes. The Systems Development manager notes that, to move to version 2, the team has to be technologically "skillful, but they didn't have to understand" the application itself because the upgrade is a technology upgrade. He comments that "we really haven't come to grips with the business side of the application very well."

While the team uses development and project management tools and procedures, it does not follow any particular methodology. The process happens as follows: the Analysis/QA manager's group analyzes requirements by going out and talking to the regions and collecting information. From that information, a functional specification is developed. The functional spec is passed on to the developers (the Systems Development manager's group), who code and test it. The code is then passed back to the Analysis/QA manager, who also manages the quality assurance team. They test the build, look for bugs, assess the build against the functional specs, and eventually okay it for production (or send it back for rework).

B. Rollout Strategies

The Credit solution will be deployed in thirty-one countries in three regions. It is replacing an existing system, which might be anything from a word processing procedure to a full-blown mainframe system. Implementation of version 2 is much more complex than the development of version 2 because it entails building an infrastructure, training, change management, interfacing with other systems, and testing. The actual implementation is a long, elaborate process in which table setups and system parameters are defined. For each site, the interface and the actual functionality are customized. The Credit solution is a flexible system.

Asia received the first version of the system because of greatest need. It was originally developed in Hong Kong for the Asian region. New York has the best technology in place and will be the last region to receive the new Credit solution. There is a need to implement in New York before 2000 to replace non-Y2K-compliant systems. According to the Implementation manager, some sites in both Asia and Europe will be completed this year because Asia is one of the fastest-growing areas in global trade in the world, followed by Eastern Europe. Therefore, both the Asia and Europe hubs will be up this year. The reason to deploy is based on the business: where it is, who is fastest growing, who has the most need, whose system is out of capacity, and whose system is barely holding on.

Implementation Process. The Implementation manager notes that "to successfully implement you have to build a partnership because it isn't possible in the silo approach to get anything done in an organization as largely diverse as the bank." The implementation process involves two steps: (1) look in the country to see how it is currently processing and its work flows and (2) deploy the system, test it, and conduct user acceptance testing. The Implementation manager espouses the "three Cs to successful project management implementation: commitment, communication, and control." The commitment is the buyin. The communication is the vehicle of keeping others and yourself informed at all times. The control is the very detailed project plan for implementation.

During the commitment phase, the Implementation manager's group makes a presentation (one or more) in the country, setting the business strategy and objectives and how the Credit solution fits in. Commitment, according to the Implementation manager, is indicated by the "country's willingness and desire to partnership with me to make this a reality," meaning that resources are made available at all stages of the implementation. This presentation is made well in advance of the actual implementation to give the regions time to adjust to the realities of the implementation. The other important role of the presentation team is to set expectations; that the way the region currently does business is going to change. The team is looking for the country to "make the commitment that you will look at your work flows and you will then sit down and have a discussion as to what we need to change in order to make this a reality for you."

There are usually several months between the presentation and implementation teams' visits to a site. When it is time to deploy the Credit solution, the implementation team then goes to the country. According to the Implementation manager:

> You go in-country and the way we do it is we send a business analyst in, a systems analyst in, we've got someone from the senior IS manager's group, the development team, the quality assurance team, to keep the global perspective so that we make sure that if any functionality changes come out of a country, we don't on a one-on-one basis make changes to the system.

The Senior IS manager travels to every country in which the company is deploying at some point. The Systems Development manager's team spends four to six weeks before, during, and after the implementation. The Analysis/QA manager also spends considerable time in the country; he's popular and in demand because he knows the system and the business.

Training. The Training manager and her two subordinates are responsible for developing the training and documentation materials and going to the country to train the trainers who will ultimately train all the users. There are 800 to 1,000 users to train, about half of whom are in New York. When the Implementation manager begins the implementation process in a country, the Training manager's group also goes (and/or it communicates with the country) to do "skills assessment": to find out what skills they have (e.g., knowledge of English and Windows, ability to manipulate a mouse). Then a training plan is developed for each country. Most of the trainers have good command of English, according to the Training manager, which is critical for their contact with the Training manager's group. The end product (letters of credit), as well as the entire system, is written in English. The Training manager guessed that the average tenure of a company technician, who is working with the letters of credit, is ten years. While these technicians' overall English language skills are not great (thus, the trainer's native language skill is important), they can handle the system and the product reasonably well.

C. Maintenance and Support Strategies
The senior IS manager does not feel that the company can do "seven by twenty-four support" out of New York alone. She anticipates that Asia will also do some support.

Starting with version 2, all changes and enhancements are handled centrally, in New York. If a site is running version 2.0, and version 2.1 contains enhancements, then that site will be upgraded to 2.1, regardless of whether the site needs the enhancements. Because its customers are global, the bank wants every site to have exactly the same level of functionality.

Changes are handled in the following way: A new request is sent around (using E-mail and *Lotus Notes*) to all regions for approval. If the change is approved as a "global" requirement, then it is incorporated into the system.

The frequency with which to do updates is a challenge. The plan is to have a major release every year, with interim releases every four or five months. The intent is that everyone will update; the Systems Development manager realizes a balance is required between the cost of too many upgrades and the cost of losing functionality (and some business opportunity).

Bug fixes are done immediately, and those fixes are incorporated into the core. Very small enhancements are likely to be treated in the same manner. A next release is scheduled when there are "ten major enhancements" (systems development manager).

IV.   Challenges and Resolutions
A. Selling the Solution
Although the firm made a conscious decision to "go global," which meant providing customers with the same look and feel wherever they interact with the firm, the focus of the Credit solution was really on technology (not business change). This occurred because of the structure and culture of the firm: a systems unit was aligned with separate business units so that when a business unit needed some technology-based solution, the firm's individual systems unit delivered it. There were few common

global applications in place. Because the firm wanted the same look and feel for letters-of-credit processing, the different business units had to cooperate to build one technology-based solution. But the lack of experience with common systems resulted in a lack of understanding of the necessity of reaching consensus on how a global common business process would work. The mentality was "this is an IS problem." Eventually, the systems people recognized an opportunity for reengineering the letters-of-credit process and for significantly streamlining it (from seventeen steps to four).

Once people recognized the need for a global system and business process, the effort to develop consensus and achieve buy in was under way. This effort was significant. There were many discussions on what it meant to be global, how the system should be developed, and where development should be located. The Analysis/QA manager said it took six months to a year to get that buy in for a global system. During that time period, there was a lot of traveling to both document current approaches to letters-of-credit processing, to build an understanding of the business process, and to build support for the global solution. But the support and commitment of senior management made the difference in helping people understand the need for change. The Analysis/QA manager remarked that people came to understand why the global solution was needed:

> We all agreed that we do need a global system. We do need to enhance our ability to provide customer service and make sure we deliver what the customer needs. The market is going forward. If we are not going to be on the cutting edge, we're going to be left behind. We all realized that. We look at other banks and other systems that they're implementing. We were behind, so we wanted to get ahead of the game.

He also noted, however, that while reaching agreement that there was a need for change, deciding on the specifics of the solution was more troublesome. In particular, determining the functional specifications for the Credit solution took considerable time and effort.

B. Managing Change

Changing letters-of-credit processing is viewed from a global perspective. The Credit solution is intended to meet customers' needs on a timely (and global) basis while incorporating local requirements. Thus, the change process includes understanding global requirements and legitimate regional or local requirements. A critical step in the process is building a partnership between the implementation team and the local site. A five-step process is used for implementing the change: defining the strategy for the local implementation, conducting the analysis of current systems and work flows, developing the solutions, implementing the solutions, and building the implementation support network.

One of the critical steps of implementation is to motivate the users to accept and commit to the change. This can be difficult. The Implementation manager argues that from the users' perspective, there is an attitude:

> "I've always done this my way; I've always done it this way. What are you going to give me that I don't have today?" So, in those cases, it's just more marketing. It's [getting users to change] really more of a sales job.

To build and sustain the relationship between the implementation team and the local sites, an inordinate amount of travel is needed. The Implementation manager is gone a minimum of two weeks a month.

To help employees learn to use the new Credit solution, a train-the-trainer approach is being used. The Training manager notes that training in a global environment is very challenging and argues that project team members need tons of patience and diplomacy. She also finds that while the trainers have knowledge of the Credit solution, they do not have in-depth, experiential knowledge of the business, which hampers their training efforts considerably.

C. Controlling and Coordinating the Process

Over the course of the project, a variety of control and coordination mechanisms is being employed. These mechanisms include two committees. There is a Global Committee, consisting of three people who indirectly report to the Senior IS manager associated with the Credit project. These three individuals are responsible for the functional requirements, and so they make decisions about what is included in the system. The second committee is a traditional Steering Committee consisting of business executives plus the senior IS manager. The norm at this firm is that the IS units associated with a particular line of business are responsible for development efforts. For the Credit project, however, the business unit is responsible.

The senior IS manager estimates that 60 percent of the control mechanisms (that is, of motivation mechanisms) are formal in nature and include compensation and flex-hour work plans. The remaining 40 percent are informal mechanisms such as team work, travel, and close communications. She notes that one of the challenges of evaluating team members is that they are compared with consultants, who are motivated by different incentives.

Several different approaches to coordination are evident. The Analysis/QA manager's group is a major coordination vehicle. In addition, coordination is accomplished through travel, conference calls, and technology such as *Lotus Notes*. *Lotus Notes* is used to control centralized change, to identify a bug, or to request an enhancement. This database is used to control the work of the developers and what goes into the next builds. While the global team uses *Notes,* the senior IS manager feels they struggle with it. She commented that requirements documents and narrative presentations are "parked in" *Notes,* but that the team has not been effective in replicating those documents on a global basis. Consequently, the team mails quite a number of the documents around. E-mail is a major coordination tool but not without drawbacks. The senior IS manager commented that though E-mail is quite effective, people tend to get inundated by the number of messages.

The Systems Development manager also uses an integrative role within his team. He has split his team functionally, including core development, interface development (for New York), Sybase function, DBA function, and infrastructure function. Once the Systems Development manager decides on monthly objectives, he assigns someone from his team to take the lead on it. That person then coordinates the activities across all persons within the Systems Development manager's group, finds and allocates resources, and so on.

D. Retaining Trained Personnel

This firm faces considerable challenges with respect to retaining qualified personnel for the project. This challenge has existed since the beginning of the project. The problem has had a negative impact on the project team's understanding of the complex requirements of the Credit solution. Consensus, with respect to system requirements, was eventually reached, and "rooms of reams of documentation" are around. However, that consensus was reached five years ago. At this point in time, people do not remember what was agreed to; some people have not even read the documentation; and there has been project personnel turnover. There are only two people associated with the project today who were involved from the beginning. Losing this continuity is rough; these are the people who remember the "spirit" of the consensus, and, while they may not remember the details, they do recall the discussion and can look at the detail. Newcomers, on the other hand, don't have that "history." Attempting to resolve this challenge, the development effort has been broken into smaller, more manageable pieces.

Keeping the developers continues to be a huge challenge. The Systems Development manager believes this is his biggest challenge. The market for these technical skills is so "hot" that the Systems Development manager has trouble keeping IS employees and consultants. He says he has "a whole slew of programmers that are VPs—not that I think that is appropriate" but to keep them, he must keep their salary competitive, which means giving them a VP title. Beyond the desire to find people with the "hot" technical skills, the Systems Development manager notes that "getting people with the right experience is hard." Many students coming out of college, he finds, have the "cowboy-PC attitude to life: just slap it in and get it done very quickly." He argues that the Credit solution application is so large and so complex that that attitude is entirely inappropriate. Moreover, he finds many college students are blown away by the complexity of the Credit solution: "I've had guys actually walk in and they walk back out, because they're Visual Basic programmers" and they have never dealt with an application of any size.

E. Managing Simultaneous Development and Deployment
Deployment is on-going while development is underway. The functional specifications for the system are built as implementations proceed. The original core system, version 1.0, was built for Hong Kong. When the next location (Singapore) was implemented, the analysts from the Analysis/QA manager's group went to Singapore and analyzed the needs there: what additional requirements are needed? The requirements were documented and sent around for global approval. Those requirements that received global approval were added to the core. Those that were not were handled in some other fashion. This same process is used each time a location is scheduled for implementation. Once the requirements are identified for a location, the Analysis/QA manager identifies an in-country business analyst who starts the more detailed analysis and documentation.

The team is also challenged by how to manage project-level change. The lack of change control procedures is problematic. How can it get code from New York to the site? Are there people in the site who can handle change control? The Systems Development manager designed a change control process that has been adopted by the entire bank. He took six months (elapsed time) to design the process.

F. Locating Development Activities and Data Processing
The development of the Credit solution system in Hong Kong, with the management in New York, was very costly. Managing the project remotely meant that decisions could not be made on a daily basis. These costs were not factored into the cost of developing the Credit solution.

When development was in Hong Kong, there were representatives from other regions (primarily New York) who participated in the requirements analysis. The understanding was that Hong Kong would develop a prototype, but the developers were not familiar with prototyping and developed a full-functioning system. By the time the other regions saw a demonstration of the Credit solution, it was beyond the point where changes could be easily accommodated. In addition, when the system came to New York from Hong Kong, it was primarily an Asian system. One of the immediate challenges was making the Credit solution more global.

Moving the development to New York was painful, according to the Systems Development manager, for several reasons: (1) the developers were starting from scratch, with no developers and no knowledge of the technology, and the application is complex; (2) the conversion to version 2 included no functionality enhancements, but the businesses did not like waiting for it, especially since Hong Kong was running an existing version; (3) the morale of Hong Kong developers was low when development was pulled away. Also, during the time when version 1 was being upgraded to version 2, if an Asian country wanted an update, the Hong Kong developers handled it and upgraded the version 1 system, and the version 2 developers incorporated that change into version 2.

Another challenge facing the firm is where to locate the data processing. The individual countries want all processing in-country; corporate headquarters wants a regional IT processing center. The resolution is a regional processing center for the servers, with all transactions being processed locally. The benefit to this arrangement is having only one UNIX expert and one Sybase expert within the region, rather than experts in each country.

G. Keeping up with "Bleeding-Edge" Technology
When the development effort was located in Hong Kong, another challenge became obvious, which was the project manager's lack of knowledge about client/server technology. She had successfully managed other types of IT projects but was not as familiar with the types of issues associated with client/server technology. Moreover, the U.S.-centered development team found that if a technology is new and "hot" in the United States, it will generally be available in Europe in six to twelve months but won't make it to Asia for another eighteen to twenty-four months. The senior IS manager noted: "We picked the newest technology we could find and we took it to the farthest reaches of the earth." She feels that New York did not really support what Asia was doing, but perhaps the bigger issue is that there is so little vendor support in Asia.

H. Addressing Cultural Differences
Cultural differences must be recognized and compensated for. For example, the U.S.-based project team found several difficulties in communicating with their Asian and European counterparts: that Asians were reluctant to say no; that many Europeans held back their opinions; and that Americans speak up (maybe too much). Working with other cultures, especially Asians, has proved challenging for this team, both with respect to development and training. The Asians were not deferential to those who were higher up in the hierarchy. The senior IS manager had difficulty with the problem solving approach of the Asians. She feels they work hard and put in lots of hours. The issue is, though, that they have lots to do and they need to learn how to better manage their time. The senior IS manager feels they need to pick what has to be done, and when they don't have the resources to do something, to raise a flag and let her know. She says their inclination is to "add another hour to a twenty-four-hour day," which is "not the solution to getting it all done." The resolution has been to try to get the Asians to share responsibility more among other countries (i.e., one country should not feel it has to do all the interface development), to give them more management responsibility to make decisions, and to provide some developmental training.

I. Working in a Global Environment

Several of the individuals involved with this project have experience working in a global environment, and that experience helps ensure that an effective global solution is deployed, as does familiarity with the technology and the business issues. The Systems Development manager had worked with global systems for the past six or seven years.. The senior IS manager and Systems Development manager both had some client/server technology experience. The Analysis/QA manager has business and IT experience. Co-locating a global team—even if the location is corporate headquarters—also facilitates the successful deployment of a global solution. Having people in the same location where they can build relationships, foster complete understanding of the issues and challenges, and work together to build the solution increases the team's ability to build the "right" system. In addition, having people on the team with varied backgrounds (including different nationalities) helps to forge a global unity. In this case, the Systems Development manager and the Analysis/QA manager are not native Americans. They are both sensitive to others' positions, and they seem to be highly respected by others.

Working in a global environment involves the challenge of time zone differences, especially between New York and Asia. Several approaches were tried to address this issue. Videoconferencing was found to be ineffective because there was no desktop videoconferencing and because participants had to be physically on the premises to access the specialized room. The facility was hard to schedule because of its popularity; this was exacerbated by the time zone differences between New York and Asia. Phones (and cell phones) proved to be much more flexible and thus more effective.

Communication on projects is always essential, but this point is brought home when working in a global environment in which languages, expectations, norms, and time zones differ. It is critical to develop active listening skills ("feeding back" according to the Systems Development manager). Phone calls cannot be the final point in an agreement; use E-mail or some other way to document the agreement. Face-to-face visits work best.

References and Suggested Readings

Air Products and Chemicals, Inc. Project ICON (A). Harvard Business School Case #9-192-097, 1992, pp. 1–21.

Air Products and Chemicals, Inc. Project ICON (B). Harvard Business School Case #9-192-102, 1992, pp. 1–2.

Air Products and Chemicals, Inc. Project ICON (C). Harvard Business School Case #9-192-106, 1992, pp. 1–2.

Air Products and Chemicals, Inc. Project ICON (D). Harvard Business School Case #9-192-089, 1994, pp. 1–13.

Appleby, Chuck. "Restructuring: The Teflon Company." *Information Week,* December 12, 1992, p. 52.

Bashein, Barbara J., M. Lynne Markus, and Jane B. Finley. *Safety Nets: Secrets of Effective Information Technology Controls.* Morristown, NJ: Financial Executives Research Foundation Inc., 1997.

Butt, Richard. "Northern Telecom Handles International HRMS With Care." *Personnel Journal* (74:6), June 1995, pp. 98–99.

Clemons, Eric K., Michael C. Row, and David B. Miller. "Rosenbluth International Alliance: Information Technology and the Global Virtual Corporation." *IEEE,* January 1992, pp. 678–686.

Deans, P. Candace, and Kirk R. Karwan. *Global Information Systems and Technology: Focus on the Organization and Its Functional Areas.* Harrisburg, PA: Idea Group Publishing, 1994.

Deans, P. Candace, and Michael J. Kane. *International Dimensions of Information Systems and Technology.* Boston, MA: PWS-Kent Publishing, 1992.

Feeny, David F., and Leslie P. Willcocks. "Core IS Capabilities for Exploiting Information Technology." *Sloan Management Review,* Spring 1998, pp. 9–21.

Fites, Donald V. "Make Your Dealers Your Partners." *Harvard Business Review* (74:2), March/April 1996, pp. 84–95.

Fryer, Bronwyn. "Allied Signal Technical Services." *Computerworld Client/Server Journal* (4:5), August 1, 1996, pp. 8–9.

Galbraith, J. R. *Designing Organizations: An Executive Briefing on Strategy, Structure, and Process.* San Francisco, CA: Jossey-Bass Inc. Publishers, 1995.

Greengard, Samuel. "When HRMS Goes Global: Managing the Data Highway." *Personnel Journal* (74:6), June 1995, pp. 90–96+.

http://www.msas.com; http://www.msas.com/unitel.html (URLs for MSAS Cargo and the Untel system)

Ives, Blake, and Sirkka L. Jarvenpaa. "MSAS Cargo International: Global Freight Management." In *Strategic Information Systems: A European Perspective.* Edited by C. Ciborra and T. Jelassi. New York: John Wiley, 1994, pp. 221–236.

Janssens, Maddy, and Jeanne M. Brett. "Coordinating Global Companies: The Effects of Electronic Communication, Organizational Commitment, and a Multi-cultural Managerial Workforce." In *Trends in Organizational Behavior,* vol 1. Edited by C. L. Cooper and D. M Rousseau. New York: John Wiley, 1994, pp. 31–46.

Kano, Nadine. *Developing International Software for Windows® 95 and Windows NT™: A Handbook for International Software Design.* Redmond, WA: Microsoft Press, 1995.

King, Julia. "Aloca Cans SAP R/3, Rolls Over to Oracle." *Computerworld,* April 29, 1996, pp. 1, 16.

Konsynski, Benn R., and Jahangir Karimi. "On the Design of Global Information Systems." In *Globalization, Technology, and Competition.* Edited by Stephen P. Bradley, Jerry A. Hausman, and Richard L. Nolan. Boston: Harvard Business School Press, 1993, pp. 81–108.

Nadler, David A. *Champions of Change: How CEOs and Their Companies Are Mastering the Skills of Radical Change.* San Francisco, CA: Jossey-Bass Inc. Publishers, 1998.

O'Hara-Devereaux, Mary, and Robert Johansen. *Global Work: Bridging Distance, Culture and Time.* San Francisco, CA: Jossey-Bass Inc. Publishers, 1994.

Palvia, Shailendra, Prashant Palvia, and Ronald M. Zigli. *The Global Issues of Information Technology Management.* Harrisburg, PA: Idea Group Publishing, 1991.

Pitkanen, Risto. "Nokia Worldwide." *Finnish Trade Review,* February 1990, p. 22

Rockart, John F., Michael J. Earl, and Jeanne W. Ross. "Eight Imperatives for the New IT Organization," *Sloan Management Review,* Fall 1996, pp. 43–55.

Ross, Jeanne W., Cynthia Mathis Beath, and Dale L. Goodhue. "Develop Long-Term Competitiveness Through IT Assets." *Sloan Management Review,* Fall 1996, pp. 31–42.

Sackman, Ralph B. *Achieving the Promise of Information Technology: Introducing the Transformational Project Paradigm.* Newtown Square, PA: Project Management Institute, 1998.

Sambamurthy, V., and Robert W. Zmud. *Information Technology and Innovation: Strategies for Success.* Morristown, NJ: Financial Executives Research Foundation Inc., 1996.

Sturken, Barbara. "Technically Speaking: Rosenbluth Travel Agency's In-House Automation System." Travel Weekly (51:13), February 13, 1992, p. 13.

Van de Ven, A. H., A. L. Delbecq, and R. Koenig Jr. "Determinants of Coordination Modes within Organizations." *American Sociological Review* (41), 1976, pp. 322–338.

Weston, Randy. "Bristol-Myers CEO Demands Massive Supply Chain Fix." *Computerworld,* November 17, 1997, pp. 47, 52.

Zmud, R. W. "Building Relationships Throughout the Corporate Entity." In *Transforming the IS Organization: The Mission, the Framework, the Transition.* Edited by J. Elam, M. Ginzberg, P. Keen, and R. Zmud. Washington, DC: ICIS Press, 1988.

About the Authors

Rosann Webb Collins, an assistant professor at the University of South Florida, received her Ph.D. in management information systems from the University of Minnesota in 1993. In addition to the deployment of global IT solutions, her research interests include the impact of information technology on knowledge work and legal and ethical issues in computing. Dr. Collins has published articles in many journals, including *MIS Quarterly, Information and Society, Journal of the American Society for Information Science, International Library Review, and the Journal of Research on Computing in Education.* She is active in many professional organizations and is a member of the Association for Information Systems and the Academy of Management.

Laurie J. Kirsch, assistant professor of business administration, joined the faculty of the Katz Graduate School of Business at the University of Pittsburgh in 1993 after completing her Ph.D. in management information systems at the University of Minnesota. Her research interests include the deployment of technology-based solutions in organizations and the impact of information technology on individuals, groups, and processes in organizations. She has published in *Organization Science, MIS Quarterly, Information Systems Research, and Accounting, Management and Information Technologies.* Dr. Kirsch is active in the International Conference on Information Systems and the Academy of Management Annual Meeting, and she belongs to the Association for Information Systems, as well as the Organizational Behavior and Organizational Communication and Information Systems divisions of the Academy of Management. Prior to her doctoral work, Dr. Kirsch spent ten years in industry, working for several Fortune 500 companies in various IS-related jobs, including technical support and project management.

Acknowledgments

The authors would like to acknowledge the help of all participating companies in this research effort. Without their cooperation, this book would not have been possible. The five case study sites, in particular, were very generous with their time, data, and insights.

The authors would also like to acknowledge the support of the Advanced Practices Council (APC) of the Society for Information Management International for funding this research project. The feedback from the members of the APC proved very useful as this research progressed through its three phases. In addition, the direction from Bob Zmud and Madeline Weiss was invaluable. Their guidance and encouragement were both needed and appreciated.

Finally, Rosann Collins would like to thank Eddie Giles, and Laurie Kirsch would like to thank Rod, William, and Noah Gasch for their patience and support these last two years. Their understanding and encouragement helped the authors to navigate the challenges and opportunities presented by this project.